W9-AFT-767

INTRODUCING
ISSUES WITH
OPPOSING
VIEWPOINTS®

Sexually Transmitted Diseases

Lauri S. Friedman and Jennifer L. Skancke, *Book Editors*

LIBRARY

GREENHAVEN PRESS
A part of Gale, Cengage Learning

GALE
CENGAGE Learning™

Detroit • New York • San Francisco • New Haven, Conn • Waterville, Maine • London

Christine Nasso, *Publisher*
Elizabeth Des Chenes, *Managing Editor*

For more information, contact:
Greenhaven Press
27500 Drake Rd.
Farmington Hills, MI 48331-3535
Or you can visit our Internet site at gale.cengage.com

Articles in Greenhaven Press anthologies are often edited for length to meet page requirements. In addition, original titles of these works are changed to clearly present the main thesis and to explicitly indicate the author's opinion. Every effort is made to ensure that Greenhaven Press accurately reflects the original intent of the authors. Every effort has been made to trace the owners of copyrighted material.

Cover image Jagged Pixel Creations/BigStockPhoto.com

LIBRARY OF CONGRESS CATALOGING-IN-PUBLICATION DATA

Sexually transmitted diseases / Lauri S. Friedman and Jennifer L. Skancke, book editors.
   p. cm. — (Introducing issues with opposing viewpoints)
  Includes bibliographical references and index.
  ISBN 978-0-7377-4174-2 (hardcover)
 1. Sexually transmitted diseases. 2. Teenagers—Sexual behavior. I. Friedman, Lauri S.
II. Skancke, Jennifer.
  RA644.V4S3735 2009
  614.5'47—dc22

                2008026732

Printed in the United States of America
1 2 3 4 5 6 7 13 12 11 10 09

Contents

Foreword

I ndulging in a wide spectrum of ideas, beliefs, and perspectives is a critical cornerstone of democracy. After all, it is often debates over differences of opinion, such as whether to legalize abortion, how to treat prisoners, or when to enact the death penalty, that shape our society and drive it forward. Such diversity of thought is frequently regarded as the hallmark of a healthy and civilized culture. As the Reverend Clifford Schutjer of the First Congregational Church in Mansfield, Ohio, declared in a 2001 sermon, "Surrounding oneself with only like-minded people, restricting what we listen to or read only to what we find agreeable is irresponsible. Refusing to entertain doubts once we make up our minds is a subtle but deadly form of arrogance." With this advice in mind, Introducing Issues with Opposing Viewpoints books aim to open readers' minds to the critically divergent views that comprise our world's most important debates.

Introducing Issues with Opposing Viewpoints simplifies for students the enormous and often overwhelming mass of material now available via print and electronic media. Collected in every volume is an array of opinions that captures the essence of a particular controversy or topic. Introducing Issues with Opposing Viewpoints books embody the spirit of nineteenth-century journalist Charles A. Dana's axiom: "Fight for your opinions, but do not believe that they contain the whole truth, or the only truth." Absorbing such contrasting opinions teaches students to analyze the strength of an argument and compare it to its opposition. From this process readers can inform and strengthen their own opinions, or be exposed to new information that will change their minds. Introducing Issues with Opposing Viewpoints is a mosaic of different voices. The authors are statesmen, pundits, academics, journalists, corporations, and ordinary people who have felt compelled to share their experiences and ideas in a public forum. Their words have been collected from newspapers, journals, books, speeches, interviews, and the Internet, the fastest growing body of opinionated material in the world.

Introducing Issues with Opposing Viewpoints shares many of the well-known features of its critically acclaimed parent series, Opposing Viewpoints. The articles are presented in a pro/con format, allowing readers to absorb divergent perspectives side by side. Active reading questions preface each viewpoint, requiring the student to approach the material thoughtfully and carefully. Useful charts, graphs, and cartoons supplement each article. A thorough introduction provides readers with crucial background on an issue. An annotated bibliography points the reader toward articles, books, and Web sites that contain additional information on the topic. An appendix of organizations to contact contains a wide variety of charities, nonprofit organizations, political groups, and private enterprises that each hold a position on the issue at hand. Finally, a comprehensive index allows readers to locate content quickly and efficiently.

Introducing Issues with Opposing Viewpoints is also significantly different from Opposing Viewpoints. As the series title implies, its presentation will help introduce students to the concept of opposing viewpoints and learn to use this material to aid in critical writing and debate. The series' four-color, accessible format makes the books attractive and inviting to readers of all levels. In addition, each viewpoint has been carefully edited to maximize a reader's understanding of the content. Short but thorough viewpoints capture the essence of an argument. A substantial, thought-provoking essay question placed at the end of each viewpoint asks the student to further investigate the issues raised in the viewpoint, compare and contrast two authors' arguments, or consider how one might go about forming an opinion on the topic at hand. Each viewpoint contains sidebars that include at-a-glance information and handy statistics. A Facts About section located in the back of the book further supplies students with relevant facts and figures.

Following in the tradition of the Opposing Viewpoints series, Greenhaven Press continues to provide readers with invaluable exposure to the controversial issues that shape our world. As John Stuart Mill once wrote: "The only way in which a human being can make some approach to knowing the whole of a subject is by hearing what can be said about it by persons of every variety of opinion and studying all modes in which it can be looked at by every character of mind. No wise man ever acquired his wisdom in any mode but this." It is to this principle that Introducing Issues with Opposing Viewpoints books are dedicated.

Introduction

Sexually transmitted diseases (STDs) are a continuous problem, one that affects more areas of the world with every passing year. Approximately 340 million new incidences of STDs, such as herpes, chlamydia, gonorrhea, syphilis, and HIV, occur each year. In one-third of those cases, the affected person is between the ages of thirteen and twenty. While the mere fact of having an STD is in itself devastating to a person's health and happiness, STDs have other far-reaching effects that include profound familial, social, professional, and economic consequences. Indeed, people with these diseases—especially if they lack access to proper treatment—can be too ill to work, which financially hurts their families and communities. Millions of children have been orphaned by the AIDS virus, forcing them to work at a young age or be thrust into prostitution or early marriage. STDs also affect future generations by causing infertility among affected women. Treating STDs and preventing their spread, therefore, is a priority not just for health-care workers but also for politicians, entrepreneurs, and many others.

But STDs have proven very difficult to treat, largely due to the poverty in many communities in which they are prevalent. Developing countries often lack the high-tech facilities and equipment needed to properly test for and treat STDs. Even though the "drug cocktails" that help control HIV have become more affordable, their $350-per-year cost is still too much for many of the affected, who may not even earn that much money in an entire year (for example, the U.S. Agency for International Development in Africa reports that the average annual income for rural Kenyans is about $360). Even when people can afford to pay for treatment, certain medicines may not always be stocked or available. As the World Health Organization has declared, "AIDS is a disease whose impact is much greater where there is poverty and social inequality, including gender inequality. It is not easily managed in settings in which weakened health systems fail to perform, especially for minorities and those living in poverty."[1]

With treatment often out of reach, the best approach for dealing with STDs in developing countries may be to focus on prevention. Developing countries are actively involved in reducing STD transmissions among their populace, often with successful results. Steve Berry, a writer for AVERT, an international HIV and AIDS charity, observes,

"Most countries in the world offer teens some sort of sexual health and HIV education in their schools at some stage."[2] Berry also notes that media education programs are an effective way of reaching adolescents who are unable to attend school because they need to work or because their parents cannot afford tuition. For example, M. Monica Sweeney and Rita Kirwan Grisman, the authors of *Condom Sense: A Guide to Sexual Survival in the New Millennium*, report that condom use has significantly reduced the number of new HIV cases in Uganda. The Ugandan government has had notable success by implementing what it calls the ABC campaign: **A**bstain from intercourse, **B**e faithful in your relationships, and use **C**ondoms.

However, Africa is not the only region determined to find solutions to the problem of STDs. AIDS is an increasingly serious issue in Asia and in the former Soviet Union, where two-thirds of affected Europeans live. Injection drug use is the primary mode of transmittal in Eastern Europe, so strategies such as providing drug users with clean needles can help reduce HIV rates. Thailand's emphasis on condom use, especially among its prostitutes and their clients, is another successful measure.

Developing nations can also seek assistance in preventing the spread of STDs from international organizations and wealthier countries, although that assistance may be limited and thus not always helpful. According to the United Nations Joint Programme on HIV/AIDS, the international community needs to spend at least $22 billion a year to successfully respond to the AIDS crisis, but actual spending has been less than half that. A greater concern for many people is that the types of programs that do get funding are ineffective. Critics of U.S. foreign policy are particularly concerned about the emphasis that America puts on abstinence education as a method of fighting STDs. While it is true that abstinence is the only surefire way to not contract a sexually transmitted disease, critics argue that the reality is that many people will be sexually active and thus need to be armed with information so they are able to practice safe sex. In addition, Berry reports that the U.S. House of Representatives found that more than 80 percent of abstinence-only education "contained false or misleading information—something that is worrying now not only for those in America but increasingly for the rest of the world, as America exports its HIV-prevention and education attitudes to parts of the world with a much higher HIV prevalence."[3] He suggests that an overreliance on abstinence education worldwide could lead to an increase in HIV figures among adolescents.

Other people dispute these criticisms, contending that studies show abstinence education has been more effective than teaching adolescents about condom use and other safe-sex practices. Stan E. Weed, who has extensively researched abstinence programs, testified before the U.S. House of Representatives Committee on Oversight and Government Reform in April 2008 that adolescents who are provided with abstinence-only education are less than half as likely as peers in other programs to engage in sexual intercourse during the following year. He states, "Emerging evidence supports the notion that abstinence-centered strategies, if well-designed and implemented, can significantly and substantially reduce teen sexual initiation for periods of 1 to 2 years."[4] The organization Concerned Women for America also cites the effectiveness of abstinence education in Uganda in reducing STD transmission. Likewise, supporters of worldwide abstinence education point out that the African countries where condoms are most readily available, such as Botswana and South Africa, actually have the highest rates of AIDS on the continent.

Because sexually transmitted diseases affect millions of teenagers and adults in the United States and worldwide, strategies for treating and preventing them will continue to be a passionately debated topic for years to come. In *Introducing Issues with Opposing Viewpoints: Sexually Transmitted Diseases*, a variety of authors from different backgrounds explore how these diseases are spread, how to prevent transmission among teenagers, and whether vaccinations are a viable solution. As the arguments above show, there is likely not one perfect solution to the problem of STDs, but some approaches may prove more effective than others.

Notes

1. World Health Organization, "HIV/AIDS: Confronting a Killer," *World Health Report*, 2003. www.who.int/whr/2003/chapter3/en/index.html.
2. Steve Berry, "Why Is AIDS Education Important for Young People?" AVERT, March 20, 2008. www.avert.org/aidsyoun.htm.
3. Berry, "Why Is AIDS Education Important for Young People?"
4. Stan E. Weed, Testimony Before the U.S. House of Representatives Committee of Oversight and Government Reform, April 23, 2008. http://oversight.house.gov/documents/20080423114465l.pdf.

Chapter 1

What Contributes to the Spread of Sexually Transmitted Diseases?

Protesters gather outside the Centers for Disease Control, criticizing President Bush's plan to expand abstinence-only education in the fight against sexually transmitted diseases.

Viewpoint

1

Abstinence-Only Education Contributes to the Spread of STDs

LeeChe Leong

"The cult of virginity that is created and perpetuated by abstinence-only education actually increases unsafe sex."

In the following viewpoint LeeChe Leong argues that abstinence-only education programs increase the spread of STDs. Abstinence-only education teaches students that the only way to avoid STDs is to remain a virgin until marriage and then to maintain a monogamous relationship thereafter. The problem with this line of thinking, says the author, is that these programs do not discuss important sexual topics such as protection or disease prevention. As such, some teens engage in sexual activities without protection, putting them at a greater risk of contracting STDs. The author concludes by saying that abstinence-only education is dangerous to teens and should be replaced with informative sex education programs.

LeeChe Leong is a contributor to *ColorLines*, a national multiracial magazine devoted to the complex issues affecting communities of color.

LeeChe Leong, "Virulent Virginity; 'Abstinence-Only' Sex Ed Programs Are Putting Youth at Risk," *ColorLines Magazine*, vol. 7, January 31, 2005, p. 36. Copyright © 2005 *ColorLines Magazine*. Reproduced by permission.

AS YOU READ, CONSIDER THE FOLLOWING QUESTIONS:
1. What does the author mean when she says that abstinence-only programs rely on "arcane notions of virginity"?
2. According to the author, virginity pledgers are how much more likely than nonpledgers to engage in unprotected sex?
3. Despite the prevalence of abstinence-only programs in high schools, what percentage of adults believe sex education should be taught instead, according to the author?

"What does penetration mean?"

The question is not that unusual in my job directing a peer education program for high school students. Yet I was taken aback because the young person who asked is sexually active. This young woman of color is just one of the millions of students misled by the sex education she has received in school.

The onslaught of federal funding for abstinence-only sex education is perpetuating a troubling trend: the rise of a virginity-based model wherein many teens are having sexual contact but not using protection. They don't think it is sex because, like former President [Bill] Clinton, they believe sex is only vaginal intercourse.

Abstinence-Only Programs Are Federally Funded

Exclusive federal funding for abstinence-only sex education began in 1996 as part of welfare reform legislation. In 2001, the Bush Administration created even more restrictive funding totaling $115 million in the past three years. Bush has requested an additional $186 million for fiscal year 2005. Approximately $100 million is now spent annually by state and federal governments on these programs, which, for lack of other federal funds, end up being the only sex education that students receive in school. States apply for the federal money, agreeing to conform to abstinence-only guidelines. Only three states, California, Arizona, and Pennsylvania, chose to not take federal funds for abstinence-only programs.

What Is Abstinence-Only Education?

According to the Department of Health and Human Services, a program is eligible when it teaches that "abstinence from sexual activity is the only certain way to avoid out-of-wedlock pregnancy, sexually transmitted diseases and other associated health problems." The program must also instruct students that "a mutually faithful monogamous relationship in the context of marriage is the expected standard of human sexual activity" and that "sexual activity outside of the context of marriage is likely to have harmful psychological and physical effects."

When these programs talk about condoms, they focus on failure rates. They ignore the existence of queer teens and never discuss what abstinence really means. Instead, the programs rely on arcane notions of "virginity," perpetuating double standards and promoting a puritanical code of silence regarding strategies for protection and prevention.

Congress has identified "Silver Ring Thing" as a model prevention program in the five-year global fight against HIV/AIDS. This self-described "faith-based abstinence message" alone received $700,000 in federal money last year to use comedy and music videos to convince middle and high school students to pledge virginity until marriage and don silver rings on their fingers as proof. Students follow up

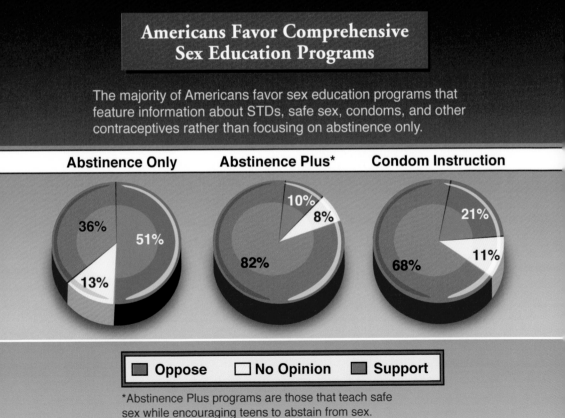

Americans Favor Comprehensive Sex Education Programs

The majority of Americans favor sex education programs that feature information about STDs, safe sex, condoms, and other contraceptives rather than focusing on abstinence only.

| Abstinence Only | Abstinence Plus* | Condom Instruction |

Abstinence Only: 36%, 51%, 13%

Abstinence Plus*: 10%, 8%, 82%

Condom Instruction: 21%, 11%, 68%

☐ Oppose   ☐ No Opinion   ☐ Support

*Abstinence Plus programs are those that teach safe sex while encouraging teens to abstain from sex.

Taken from: A. Bleakley et al., "Public Opinion on Sex Education in U.S. Schools," *Archives of Pediatrics and Adolescent Medicine*, vol. 160, no. 11, November 2006.

with an abstinence Bible study. Conveniently, a "second virginity" is offered to those who have been sexually active in the past. The Silver Ring Thing website lists the names of sexually transmitted infections and pregnancy rates for girls eight times on their statistics page; they mention boys once. There is no mention of condoms.

Abstinence-Only Programs Misinform Teens About Sex

While called "abstinence-only," the programs are in essence virginity-based and they pride themselves on not addressing the "graphic terms better left to parents to discuss." In doing so the programs leave the door open for teens to make unsafe sexual choices while operating under the belief that they are still virgins. The ranks of those "saving themselves" by being blowjob queens are increasing as oral sex is on the rise. While oral sex is most prevalent among white teens, it is young black men between 15 and 17 who report the greatest increase in one longitudinal study, jumping from 25 percent in 1988 to 57 percent in 1995, the last year rates were reported in the National Survey of Adolescent Males.

Many teens say that oral sex does not count as sex. Of those who describe themselves as "not sexually active," 13 percent report having oral sex, according to the National Survey of Adolescents and Young Adults. And almost 30 percent of Latino teens consider oral sex to be "safer sex," according to the survey. Nearly half of those who are sexually active consider oral sex the "safer sex." Teens believe oral sex is "not as big a deal" as sexual intercourse. More disturbingly, sexually active girls are twice as likely as sexually active boys to report having had oral sex to avoid intercourse.

STDs in Teens Are on the Rise

Sexually transmitted infection rates continue to rise among adolescents, disproportionately affecting teens in communities of color.

Recent health campaigns promote abstaining from sex, but such advertisements may not be an effective method for today's teenagers to follow.

In 2001, the chlamydia rate for 15- to 19-year-olds was 12 times higher among black men than among white men; the rate among black women of the same age was nearly seven times higher than among white women. According to Sexually Transmitted Disease Surveillance, the gonorrhea rate in 2002 for black men, ages 15 to 19, was 45 times higher than that of white men; black women of the same age had a rate 17 times that of white women. Native Americans had nearly 4 times the rate of non-Hispanic whites and Latinos had over twice the rate. Rather than address these numbers, public policy pundits have applauded the 35 percent decrease in the teen birth rate among 15- to 17-year-olds, principally celebrating the 46 percent drop among black teens.

Abstinence-Only Education Increases Unsafe Sex

The cult of virginity that is created and perpetuated by abstinence-only education actually increases unsafe sex. A five year study of 12,000 adolescents aged 12 to 18 found that sex without protection

This map represents how an STD would spread over eighteen months of hook-ups and breakups at a Midwestern high school. Boys are in blue, girls are in pink, and they are connected by the possibilities for viral transmission. Dark blue lines indicate that two students can infect each other through shared lovers, while gray arrows represent one-way transmission. Researchers found the possibility for infection was so high it could be classified as a "recipe for an epidemic."

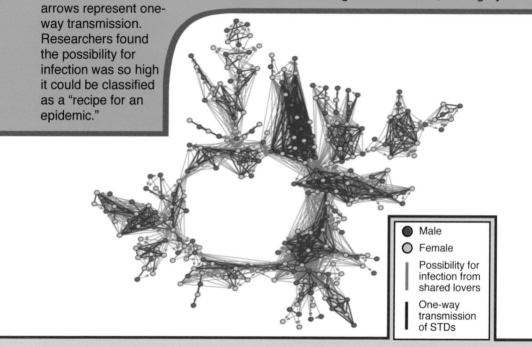

Male
Female
Possibility for infection from shared lovers
One-way transmission of STDs

Taken from: Stephen Ornes, "Teens Make Life Easy for STDs," Discover, June 18, 2007.

is a third more likely among young people who signed virginity-until-marriage pledges. Peter Bearman, a sociology professor at Columbia University and co-author of the study, told the Associated Press, "It's difficult to simultaneously prepare for sex and say you're not going to have sex."

According to Bearman, 88 percent of those pledging virginity reported having sex before marriage. They delayed activity only 18 months more than those not pledging. Rates of sexually transmitted infections were similar between the groups because those making virginity pledges are much less likely to use condoms. Nearly half of black 15- to 17-year-olds report having used the withdrawal method as birth control or protection.

In addition to the "virginal" teens having oral sex, 30 percent of those who self-identified as "not sexually active" report having been "intimate" in some way. The prohibition on information perpetuated by virginity-based programs leaves sexually active teens unprotected and wondering what penetration means.

Research on young adults suggests that such substitute activities rarely include protection. While 84 percent of U.S. adults, ages 18 to 35, say they take "necessary" steps to protect themselves against sexually transmitted diseases, 82 percent of participants said they don't use protection during oral sex. Despite the increased risk of infection, 64 percent do not use protection during anal sex.

Sex Education Needs to Be Taught

Poverty, incarceration rates and a lack of access to health care are all obstacles to treatment and all disproportionately affect communities of color. Adolescents need to know what services are available and where they can access them. They need to know what rights they have. Parents recognize this: 93 percent of adults support sexuality education in high school. Bush's own surgeon general has stated that sex education needs to include condoms and other types of birth control.

Despite the fact that adolescents experience nearly 4 million cases of sexually transmitted infections annually in the United States—nearly two-thirds of all cases—the Bush administration continues to promote and exclusively fund dangerous virginity-based models.

EVALUATING THE AUTHOR'S ARGUMENTS:

In the viewpoint you just read, LeeChe Leong argues that abstinence-only sex education programs contribute to the spread of STDs. What pieces of evidence does she use to support this claim? Did she convince you of her argument? Explain why or why not.

Viewpoint

2

Declining Morals Contribute to the Spread of STDs

Johannes L. Jacobse

"The [STD] crisis exists because society has jettisoned the moral standards that direct sexual behavior."

In the following viewpoint Johannes L. Jacobse argues that the decline of society's morals has increased the spread of STDs. He explains that sexual promiscuity is heavily featured, and even encouraged, in American television, film, and magazines. As a result, more and more people—and especially teens—are engaging in sex than ever before. In fact, it has become common practice to have sex outside of marriage, have multiple partners, and engage in deviant sexual behavior. With increased sexual activity comes increased exposure to STDs, the author claims. In order to prevent the spread of STDs, the author concludes, society needs to adjust its moral values by preventing marketers from selling sex and desexualizing American culture.

Johannes L. Jacobse is a Greek Orthodox priest and edits the Orthodoxy Today Web site.

Fifteen year old Laurie was rushed to the emergency room with acute pain in her lower abdomen. Doctors initially suspected appendicitis but during surgery they discovered something worse. Laurie suffered from pelvic inflammatory disease that was caused by either chlamydia or gonorrhea. The infection began in her cervix, then climbed through the uterus into her fallopian tubes and out to her ovaries. An abscess that formed on her right ovary had ruptured, spilling the infection into her abdominal cavity. Quick action by the surgeons saved Laurie's life but she will probably never bear children.

Laurie's story is one of many that illustrate the pages of Meg Meeker's "Epidemic: How Teen Sex Is Killing Our Kids." A pediatrician who has treated teens for over two decades, Meeker sounds the alarm about the epidemic of sexually transmitted diseases (STDs) that is killing our kids.

Teens Face an STD Epidemic

An epidemic is defined as a disease that attacks many people simultaneously. During an epidemic the incidence of the disease grows, and the disease attacks areas where it would otherwise not be found—such as the bodies of young children. The STD epidemic is even more dangerous because it involves more than one disease. The Centers for Disease Control and Prevention in Atlanta categorizes the STD crisis as a *multiple epidemic* since it consists of at least 25 different STDs—50 if you count the variant strains of the same disease.

The epidemic is so large that it becomes difficult to grasp how serious it is. Imagine flying over Yellowstone National Park at 10,000 feet. Looking out the window we see thousands of small fires dotting the park. Some of the fires are blazing, some smoldering, some are

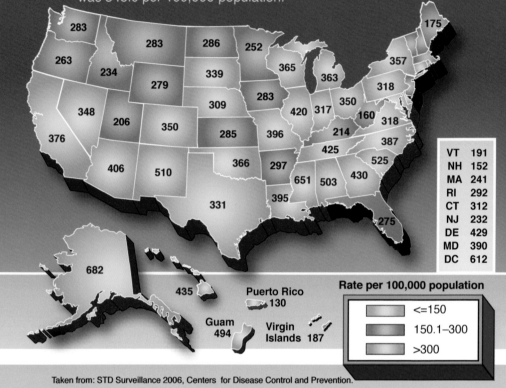

Chlamydia Rates by State

In 2006 the total rate of chlamydia for the United States and outlying areas (Guam, Puerto Rico, and Virgin Islands) was 345.0 per 100,000 population.

VT	191
NH	152
MA	241
RI	292
CT	312
NJ	232
DE	429
MD	390
DC	612

Puerto Rico 130
Guam 494
Virgin Islands 187

Rate per 100,000 population
<=150
150.1–300
>300

Taken from: STD Surveillance 2006, Centers for Disease Control and Prevention.

just a trace of smoke and a few sparks. On the ground we see one or two, maybe three fires. From the air the fires are spreading and threaten to engulf the entire park. This is the danger of STDs in the teen population.

How Many Teens Have STDs?

Another illustration shows how many teens are affected. Imagine a high school football stadium filled with teenagers. Then start counting. One in five of the cheering kids has herpes. Herpes has no cure. Every third girl has the human papilloma virus (HPV). HPV causes 99.7% of cervical cancer cases that kills over 5000 women each year. One out of ten has chlamydia. Even if we pulled out the healthy kids, the stadium would still be nearly full.

Consider these statistics:

- Almost half of all students in grades nine through twelve have had sex.
- Half of all girls are likely to be infected with an STD during their first sexual experience.
- Nearly one in four of sexually active teens has an STD.
- Teens will contract nearly one in four of the 15 million new cases of STDs this year.
- Teens make up 10% of the population but contract up to 25% of all STDs.
- Herpes (specifically herpes simplex type 2 or "genital herpes") has skyrocketed 500% among white teenagers in the last 20 years.
- One in five children above age twelve tests positive for herpes type 2.
- One in ten teenage girls has chlamydia, and half of all new chlamydia cases each year are diagnosed in girls 15 to 19 years old.

It gets worse. The *Journal of the American Medical Association* reported in a February 2002 editorial that the number of people with asymptomatic STDs (diseases with no outward symptoms like lesions or warts) probably exceeds those whose diseases are diagnosed. This means that the epidemic may be twice as large as we think.

STDs Are Hurting Teens

The STD epidemic is a catastrophe. Millions of teens have been hurt. Millions more are threatened. Diseases are tearing into the bodies of our children in ways that will cause irreparable harm or even kill them.

The crisis exists because society has jettisoned the moral standards that direct sexual behavior. The shift began with the "sexual revolution" in the sixties when the effects of unbridled promiscuity were largely unknown. (Only two known STDs existed thirty years ago both treatable with penicillin.) As society adopted the values of the sixties the moral culture changed. Promiscuity ruled the day and STDs spread like wildfire.

Big media is a big culprit because they target teens with the message that sex has no risks. They have sexualized almost every corner of the youth culture. They relentlessly sell promiscuity but make no mention of the harm that the promiscuity causes. They care for your child's wallet but not for his welfare. Greed drives their moral recklessness.

Parents Must Protect Teens from STDs

There are things that parents can do. Several years ago the Search Institute, a Minneapolis-based think tank that studies the moral lives of children, isolated three factors in the lives of teens who successfully

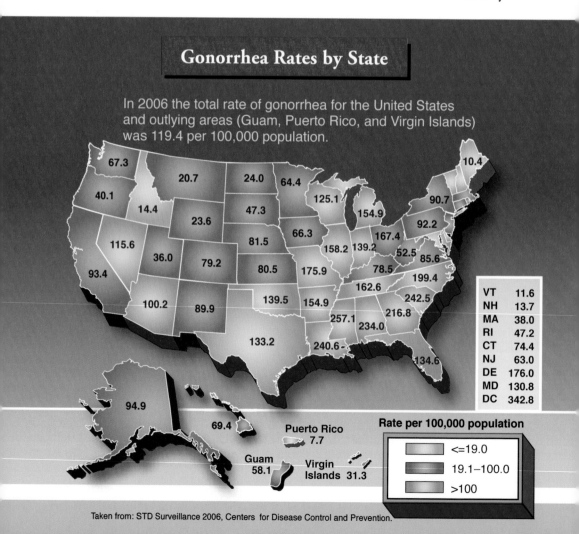

Gonorrhea Rates by State

In 2006 the total rate of gonorrhea for the United States and outlying areas (Guam, Puerto Rico, and Virgin Islands) was 119.4 per 100,000 population.

| 67.3 | | | | | | | 10.4 |

20.7 24.0 64.4 125.1 90.7
40.1 14.4 47.3 154.9 92.2
23.6 66.3 167.4
115.6 81.5 158.2 139.2 52.5 85.6
36.0 79.2 80.5 175.9 78.5 199.4
93.4 162.6
100.2 89.9 139.5 154.9 242.5
257.1 216.8
133.2 234.0
240.6 134.6
94.9 69.4

VT	11.6
NH	13.7
MA	38.0
RI	47.2
CT	74.4
NJ	63.0
DE	176.0
MD	130.8
DC	342.8

Puerto Rico 7.7

Rate per 100,000 population

Guam 58.1

Virgin Islands 31.3

	<=19.0
	19.1–100.0
	>100

Taken from: STD Surveillance 2006, Centers for Disease Control and Prevention.

Pictured is the cast of Sex and the City, *a popular cable television show that followed the relationships and sexual adventures of four female friends.*

navigated the minefield of teen culture. The teens who developed sound morality and avoided non-marital sex and other enticements of the teen culture had three things working for them: 1) a relationship with a stable adult in addition to their parents; 2) friends who shared the same moral values; and 3) a religious grounding. Parents must cultivate this kind of environment.

Parents must be vigilant. Parents should listen to the music their children hear, watch the same television shows, read the same magazines, and rent the same movies. When parents encounter something objectionable, they need to explain to their teen what is wrong with the product and not allow it in the home. Teens may object and resist, but deep down they will be grateful that the parent stands up for what is right.

Parents must educate themselves. Don't be swayed by arguments that characterize teens as incapable of morally responsible behavior. The latest research shows that sex-education programs that promote "safe sex" have no effect on reducing teenage sexual activity. "Abstinence only" programs however, have cut sexual activity—by over 50% in places—depending on the program.

Be alert to misrepresentations of the risks associated with sexual activity such a the "safe sex" campaign. Safe sex is a myth. Condoms

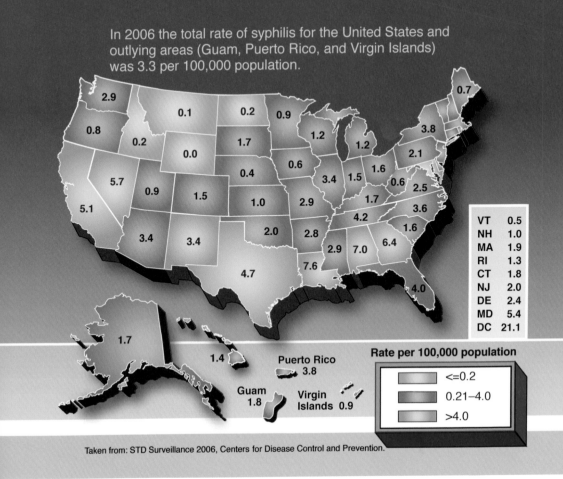

Syphilis Rates by State

In 2006 the total rate of syphilis for the United States and outlying areas (Guam, Puerto Rico, and Virgin Islands) was 3.3 per 100,000 population.

VT	0.5	
NH	1.0	
MA	1.9	
RI	1.3	
CT	1.8	
NJ	2.0	
DE	2.4	
MD	5.4	
DC	21.1	

Puerto Rico 3.8

Guam 1.8

Virgin Islands 0.9

Rate per 100,000 population

<=0.2	
0.21–4.0	
>4.0	

Taken from: STD Surveillance 2006, Centers for Disease Control and Prevention.

can reduce the incidence of fluid borne STDs but have no effect on diseases spread by skin-to-skin contact such as herpes. Even the reduction of fluid borne diseases is much less than most people think. Gonorrhea, for example, is spread 50% of the time even when a condom is correctly used. Birth control pills can prevent pregnancy but are powerless against every kind of STD.

"Sexual Purity Needs to Be Cultivated"

Note too that most organizations that promote safe sex are those that market promiscuity or profit from its consequences. Moral responsibility is not part [of] the MTV, Abercrombie and Fitch, *Cosmo Girl* or Planned Parenthood corporate culture, for example. Safe-sex campaigns give an appearance of moral respectability but avoid real moral accountability.

Meeker writes that her two-decade practice with teens has taught her that most teens have a deep-seated desire to protect their virginity. Priests who work with teens report the same thing. This is one reason why many teens experience deep anguish after their first sexual encounter. They sense that something important has been lost. This desire for sexual purity needs to be cultivated and affirmed.

What else works to reduce teen STD rates? Recent research (through 2006) suggests that abortion parental notification laws curb teen sexual activity thereby slowing the rate of the STD epidemic. Teens don't want their parents to find out they are sexually active so they engage in sexual behavior much less. The analysts need to study the data a lot more but common sense tells us something too: give teens a solid reason to say no to sexual activity, and some will find a way to resist the sexualization of the youth culture that morally irresponsible adults foist upon them.

Teens are desperate for moral guidance. They need protectors, especially from the marketers who deliver a harmful poison in their promises of acceptance and love through sexual promiscuity.

EVALUATING THE AUTHOR'S ARGUMENTS:

The author of this viewpoint, Johannes L. Jacobse, is a Greek Orthodox priest. Does knowing the background of the author influence your opinion of his argument? In what way?

Prostitution Contributes to the Spread of STDs

"Experts consider prostitutes to be 'core transmitters' [of STDs] because of their high infection rates and large numbers of partners."

Jonathan Bor

In the following viewpoint author Jonathan Bor discusses how prostitution contributes to the spread of STDs in America. He explains that women who sell sex for money and drugs are at a high risk of contracting an STD because they have sex with a lot of people and do not always use protection. Such behavior makes their chances of becoming infected with an STD very high, says Bor. Furthermore, STDs spread beyond local sex-trade areas to suburban and rural areas when customers bring STDs back to their own communities. The author concludes that prostitution is a health hazard for sex workers and the general public.

Jonathan Bor is a reporter for the *Baltimore Sun,* a Maryland-based newspaper from which this viewpoint was taken.

AS YOU READ, CONSIDER THE FOLLOWING QUESTIONS:

1. How high does the author say STD infection rates are among prostitutes in the United States?

2. According to the author, what percentage of prostitutes infected with HIV engage in unprotected sex?
3. How do STDs spread from the city sex trade to outlying suburban areas, as explained by the author?

While just a teenager in the 1970s, she danced on The Block, where she snorted cocaine and heroin and sold sex in back rooms. Later, with her addictions firmly rooted, she set out on her own, offering her body on the streets of West Baltimore as a deadly virus was spreading.

Prostitutes Are "Core Transmitters" of STDs

The years have worn away at Sharon Williams, whose deeply lined face, reddened eyes and pained expressions tell of poor health, nights in abandoned buildings and customers like the man who kicked her down a flight of stairs, breaking two ribs and puncturing a lung.

Yet she remained a prostitute to support herself and her habits. Not even the discovery 12 years ago that she had been infected with HIV changed that. She also counts herself among the many addicted women who, despite knowing the risks, have given in to customers who refuse to wear condoms.

"They'll do anything for a high," Williams said. "If they want money enough, they'll agree to it. I've slipped up once in a while."

The sale of sex for drug money is an important but largely overlooked reason why Baltimore has the nation's second-highest rate of AIDS diagnoses, trailing only Miami. By the end of [2006] almost 16,000 city residents were living with HIV or AIDS.

Women desperate for their next fix and men willing to risk their health for cheap sex are partners in an epidemic that shows no signs of ending. Experts consider prostitutes to be "core transmitters" because of their high infection rates and large numbers of partners. . . .

"The Trading of Sex and Drugs"

Public health authorities have been slow to address the connection between AIDS and what some experts call "survival sex," in part because the people involved are elusive and their role hard to quantify. Most of the women have been addicted to drugs and, in some cases, ensnared in prostitution since childhood. Many are homeless, wandering from one abandoned building to another.

A key part of the sex trade, epidemiologists say, is crack cocaine. The drug produces an intense high followed quickly by a crushing depression that can be relieved only by smoking more. Crack, which has been a major presence in Baltimore since the early 1990s, drives many female addicts into a relentless cycle of drug-seeking and prostitution.

"They have a lot of partners to sustain their habits," said Dr. Jacques Normand, chief of the AIDS program at the National Institute on Drug Abuse. "There is no question in this country that there's a substantial epidemiological relationship between crack and HIV transmission. It all comes down to the trading of sex and drugs."

Terry Brown, vice president of Baltimore Behavioral Health, daily sees the link between drug use and prostitution among the women who enter his drug treatment center. "I would say that if we have a woman who is a substance abuser, is unemployed and has no income, the way she supports her habit is the sex trade," said Brown, who is co-chairman of the city's Commission on HIV/AIDS Prevention and Treatment. . . .

As women selling sex for drugs, many have been routinely exposed to beatings, robberies and sexually transmitted diseases, including HIV. . . .

STD Risk Rises with Prostitution

Among women who trade sex, studies find infection rates as high as 30 percent in locales around the nation. Such studies haven't been done in Baltimore, though several nonprofit groups that serve this population report rates that are similar or higher.

In general, the odds of an infected woman spreading the virus to a man through sex are lower than the odds of a man transmitting HIV to a woman. For female-to-male transmission, the risk might be as low as one in 1,000 for a single act of intercourse.

But the risk rises steeply if certain conditions are met. A woman with a genital sore is more contagious. An uncircumcised man is more susceptible. A woman who has gone untreated might have more virus to shed.

The risk, studies have shown, can rise as high as one in four, depending on which conditions are met.

Prostitutes are called "core transmitters" due in part to their high number of sexual partners.

"The likelihood they will infect someone keeps going up because of the probabilities," said Dr. Thomas Quinn, infectious disease professor at the Johns Hopkins Bloomberg School of Public Health. "If the odds are one out of 10 and someone has sex with 10 people, then one is going to get infected."

Many of those who trade sex for drugs have sexually transmitted infections such as syphilis, gonorrhea and chlamydia, which boost their susceptibility to HIV—and the potential to pass it along. People who have lesions caused by these infections are three to six times more likely to spread the virus in a single act of sex, according to experts.

"Their primary focus is on getting high," said Dr. Jonathan Zenilman, chief of infectious diseases at Johns Hopkins' Bayview Medical Center. "They may ignore symptoms of STIs [sexually transmitted infections], ulcerations. They are chronically ill, a lot of them.". . .

Unprotected Sex Spreads STDs

The link between crack, risky sex and the virus has not been well-studied in Baltimore. But in Miami, which has the nation's highest AIDS rate, a study among female crack addicts provides some insight.

There, the drug of choice is overwhelmingly crack, in contrast to Baltimore, where heroin and crack addiction are intertwined. But the Miami experience shows the role that crack can play in motivating prostitutes to seek one customer after another, said Dr. Toya Brewer of the University of Miami.

> ### FAST FACT
>
> The organization AVERT reports that prostitutes who inject drugs are as much as six times more likely to be HIV-positive.

Brewer set out to measure sexual risk-taking among female crack addicts. A majority had at least one paying customer. Three-quarters who were HIV-negative engaged in unprotected sex. Among those who were positive, 56 percent had unprotected sex—a smaller percentage, but a majority nonetheless.

Sex-trading addicts draw customers from inside and outside their social circles. "They can be linked to people who are not in their group who in turn spread HIV in the larger community," Brewer said. "Some of them are exposing others; the rest are exposing themselves.". . .

Reducing Prostitution Is Challenging

Prostitution, which has a long history in Baltimore, increased noticeably with the arrival of crack in the 1990s. Public health authorities believe that it triggered a syphilis outbreak, which they eventually quelled by offering testing and antibiotics in the worst drug neighborhoods.

But reducing prostitution was far more difficult. Dr. Peter L. Beilenson, then the city health commissioner, said he is convinced that the sex-for-drugs trade was one of the main forces driving the HIV epidemic during his 13-year tenure.

"They're not an easy group to reach," he said. "They're not all in the Route 40 corridor or even in hotel rooms, where some of the prostitution occurs."

The city sex trade ripples beyond the neighborhoods where it is concentrated. Just as people drive into the city for drugs, men from outlying areas cruise the streets for sex, running the risk of becoming infected and passing the virus to their spouses or other partners.

Prostitution Is a Vicious Cycle

How many women who sell sex in Baltimore remains unknown although advocates for them contend that there could be thousands. About 700 visit two drop-in centers, and 1,000 prostitution cases are filed annually in District Court. That number probably includes multiple cases for some women, according to a prosecutor. On the other hand, many go undetected.

Some women don't work the streets at all, trading sex instead with male drug dealers and acquaintances. Some accept as little as $5 but say they are frequently offered more for sex without a condom. The women are engaged in a relentless if dangerous struggle—not only for drugs but also for the necessities of life.

"It could be for money, food or clothing," said Dr. Susan Sherman, a Johns Hopkins epidemiologist who refers to their work [as] "survival sex." "It could be for cigarettes, drugs, anything."

EVALUATING THE AUTHOR'S ARGUMENTS:

Jonathan Bor quotes from several sources to support the points he makes in his essay. Make a list of everyone he quotes, including their credentials and the nature of their comments. Then analyze his sources—are they credible? Are they well qualified to speak on the subject?

Viewpoint
4

Regulated Prostitution Does Not Contribute to the Spread of STDs

"Currently there are 26 operational HIV prevention projects among different sections of the society."

Isaac C-H Fung et al.

In the following viewpoint, a study was conducted among commercial sex workers in Ahmedabad, which is an industrial city in Gujarat, India. The goal of the study was to regulate prostitution and thus reduce the spread of STDs. In the fifty-one-month study, there was a decrease in STDs, such as HIV, among the prostitutes in Ahmedabad. Providing sex workers with frequent medical exams and educating on consistent condom use was the key success of the STD decline in Ahmedabad. Furthermore, this viewpoint expresses that reducing the number of STDs in prostitutes helps prevent the diseases from spreading into the general population. Regulating prostitution, the authors argue, can positively impact the health of society as a whole.

Isaac C-H Fung et al., "Modelling the Impact and Cost-Effectiveness of the HIV Intervention Programme Amongst Commerical Sex Workers in Ahmedabad, Gujarat, India," *BMC Public Health*, vol. 7, August 6, 2007. Copyright © Fung et al.; licensee BioMed Central Ltd. Reproduced by permission.

Isaac C-H Fung is one of the managing editors of the journal *Emerging Themes in Epidemiology*. He works in the Department of Infectious Disease Epidemiology at Imperial College London.

AS YOU READ, CONSIDER THE FOLLOWING QUESTIONS:
1. How many people in India were living with HIV in 2005?
2. What are the four main strategies for reducing HIV transmission according to the study?
3. Over the fifty-one months, how many condoms were distributed in Jyoti Sangh?

The HIV epidemic in India is no longer negligible, with an estimated 5.7 million people living with HIV in 2005 (0.91% of the adult population). Although the overall prevalence in India may be below 1%, in the southern states of Andhra Pradesh, Karnataka and Maharashtra, and the north-eastern states of Manipur and Nagaland, the ante-natal clinic prevalence is above 1%. In Gujarat the prevalence is generally much lower (0.13% among ante-natal clinic attendees in 2004). However, in the city of Ahmedabad, the HIV prevalence in 2003 amongst ante-natal clinic attendees was 0.75%, and was 13.2% amongst CSWs [commercial sex workers]. This is particularly concerning since Ahmedabad is the seventh largest city in India with a population of over 4.5 million in 2005.

HIV Prevention Projects

Under guidance and support from the Ahmedabad Municipal Corporation AIDS Control Society (AMCACS), HIV prevention programmes in Ahmedabad started in 1997. Currently there are 26 operational HIV prevention projects among different sections of the society. One of these is the CSW prevention project run by Jyoti Sangh, a non-governmental organisation that promotes the welfare and empowerment of women. This project is supported by the Department for International Development, UK, and is an integral part of the National AIDS Control Programme implemented across India under the guidance of NACO.

Jyoti Sangh has contact with CSWs from different areas of the city that work on the street and in other settings such as brothels and beauty parlours. Their four main strategies for reducing HIV transmission include: (1) Increase the knowledge of HIV/AIDS and sexually transmitted infections (STI) among CSW; (2) Improve the STI treatment of CSW and their clients; (3) Increase safer sex practices among CSW; and (4) Provide an environment that enables CSWs and the sex industry to promote safe sex behaviours. Outreach workers, assisted by peer educators, visit CSWs regularly to distribute condoms, promote safer sex practices and encourage CSWs to attend the free STI clinic. Using snowballing methods, Jyoti Sangh estimated that there are 4,000 (range 3,500–4,500) CSWs in Ahmedabad, and that since 1998, the number of CSWs reached by them has increased from 400 to over 3,050 in 2004.

Safe-Sex Methods Decrease the Spread of STDs

In order to evaluate the impact of the Jyoti Sangh HIV prevention programme on sexual risk behaviour and prevalence of HIV and other STIs, two surveys were undertaken in August/September 1999 and November/December 2003. The surveys assessed the laboratory prevalence of *Chlamydia trachomtis, Neisseria gonorrhoea,* syphilis and *Trichomonas vaginalis,* and HIV, along with their behavioural correlates, such as condom usage and the number of clients per day. Over the 51 months between these surveys, Jyoti Sangh distributed over 5.5 million condoms. In addition, from January 2001 to December 2003, on average 2,342 CSWs were reached per month and 58 people were treated for STDs by the free clinic (range: 5 to 221 per month). Compared to the 1999 survey, the 2003 survey demonstrated a significant decrease in the prevalence of treatable STIs and a stabilisation of the HIV prevalence; this was reflected in a significant decrease in the reported number of sexual partners and a significant increase in consistent condom use.

This study aims to evaluate the Jyoti Sangh HIV intervention programme by using mathematical modelling and cost-effectiveness analysis with setting-specific epidemiological, behavioural and intervention data. The impact of the intervention is estimated in terms of HIV cases averted amongst CSW and their clients, and its cost-effectiveness as Indian rupees (INR) and US dollars (USD) per HIV case averted. . . .

Effective Results

There were 119 runs that fit the survey data of HIV prevalence amongst CSWs in 2003 and STI prevalence amongst CSWs in 1999 and 2003. These model fits project that the intervention averted 624 (Uncertainty range: 310–1,191) HIV infections amongst CSWs in Ahmedabad from the beginning of September 1999 to the end of November 2003 (51 months)—53.8% (Uncertainty range: 38.4%–68.8%) of the HIV

Registered sex workers' health cards are inspected for biweekly screenings by a city health inspector.

infections that would have occurred without the intervention. In contrast, 5,131 (Uncertainty range: 2,282–8,896) HIV infections were averted among clients—51.2% (Uncertainty range: 33.4%–64.1%) of those that would have occurred. . . .

The intervention resulted in a reduction in the STI prevalence amongst the clients and commercial sex workers, which would have been stable otherwise. Indeed, if there had been no intervention, the HIV prevalence in December 2003 would have been 25.7% (Uncertainty range: 16.5%–39.4%) among CSWs and 3.1% (Uncertainty range: 1.4%–5.7%) among clients, nearly twice as high as the observed and projected HIV prevalences amongst CSWs and clients in 2003 with the intervention (1.6%, Uncertainty range: 0.9%–2.9% for clients). The model estimates that the STI prevalence of clients in the absence of intervention would have been 8.1% (Uncertainty range: 4.5%–12.2%), compared to 4.1% (Uncertainty range: 2.21%–4.35%) in the presence of intervention. Without the intervention, the model projects that the overall CSWs STI prevalence would have remained stable at 75.5%. . . .

This study demonstrated that targeted CSW interventions in India can be cost-effective, and highlights the importance of replicating this effort in other similar settings. This impact study can be used as a reference from which to compare the impact of other intervention programmes in India.

EVALUATING THE AUTHORS' ARGUMENTS:

In this viewpoint, the authors and researchers of the study conducted in India showed that regulating prostitution and educating sex workers decreased the spread of STDs. Do you think a similar study and education program is needed in the United States? Do you think U.S. citizens would support such a program? Why or why not? Explain your reasoning using evidence from the text and what you know about this topic.

Homosexuality Contributes to the Spread of STDs

Traditional Values Coalition

"Homosexual sex leads to serious venereal diseases . . . and death from HIV infection."

In the following viewpoint the Traditional Values Coalition argues that homosexuality is the reason behind the increased number of STD infections in America. According to the author, homosexuals engage in dangerous sex acts, such as unprotected oral and anal sex, that put them at a high risk of contracting an STD. In fact, the author says that homosexuals are acquiring STDs such as hepatitis B, gonorrhea, human papillomavirus (HPV), and syphilis in record numbers. This behavior is a threat not only to the gay community but also to the general public that has intimate contact with infected homosexuals. To thwart the spread of STDs, the author urges that homosexual behavior be discouraged.

The Traditional Values Coalition is an interdenominational public policy organization speaking on behalf of more than forty-three thousand churches.

Traditional Values Coalition, "Homosexual Behavior Fuels AIDS and STD Epidemic," *Traditional Values Coalition,* December 2003. Reproduced by permission.

AS YOU READ, CONSIDER THE FOLLOWING QUESTIONS:
1. According to the author, what health risks come from homosexual behavior?
2. How does the author explain the increasing rate of HIV/AIDS among homosexuals?
3. By how much have syphilis rates increased in the Southern California gay population, according to the author?

The Centers for Disease Control (CDC) announced on November 26, 2003, that AIDS infections increased in 29 states in 2002 among Blacks, Latinos, and Homosexual and Bisexual men. The overall rate of increase was 5.1% over a four-year period between 1999–2002. Fifty-five percent of these infections are among Blacks; there was a 26% increase among Latinos; and a 17% increase among homosexuals and bisexuals. There was a 7% increase in AIDS infections among nonhomosexuals. . . .

Homosexual Behavior Is Unhealthy

Dr. John Diggs, Jr., has recently published statistics on the serious health consequences of engaging in homosexual sodomy. . . .

Dr. Diggs notes that homosexual sodomy is an efficient transmitter of a whole range of STDs including AIDS. He also points out that human physiology makes it clear that anal intercourse itself is an unhealthy practice that damages the body and can lead to serious health consequences—including anal cancer. *"Unhealthy sexual behaviors occur among both heterosexuals and homosexuals. Yet the medical and social science evidence indicate that homosexual behavior is uniformly unhealthy,"* observes Diggs.

The sexual activities engaged in by homosexuals inevitably lead to a whole range of viral and bacterial infections that can result in sterility, cancer, and death. . . .

Homosexuals Engage in Dangerous Sex Acts

One of the largest surveys ever conducted of homosexual sex practices was published by two homosexual researchers in 1979. In *The Gay Report* by Jay and Young, 37% of homosexuals interviewed indicated they had engaged in sadomasochistic activities; 23% had been involved in "water sports" (urinating on the sex partner); 4% had been involved in defecation; and 11% had been involved in giving enemas to their sex partners.

Homosexuality Spreads Disease

Dr. Gisela L.P. Macphail, a physician at the University of Calgary in Canada, described the serious health risks of homosexual behavior in a letter to the Calgary Board of Education in September, 1996. She is an epidemiologist and regularly treats AIDS patients. According to Dr. Macphail, "Any practice which facilitates direct or indirect oral-rectal contact will enable the spread of fecal and rectal microorganisms to the sexual partner. Thus anilingus (rimming), a common practice among homosexual men, allows direct spread of pathogens such as

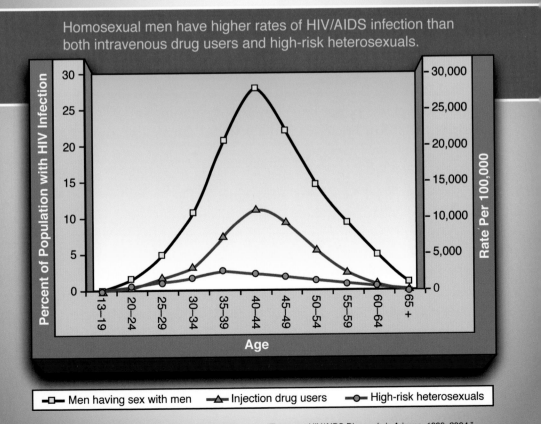

Gay Men Are at High Risk for HIV/AIDS

Homosexual men have higher rates of HIV/AIDS infection than both intravenous drug users and high-risk heterosexuals.

Taken from: Arizona Department of Health Services, "Emergent HIV/AIDS Diagnosis in Arizona, 1999–2004."

Giardia, *Entamoeba histolytica,* and Hepatitis A and of the typical STD organisms such as herpes simplex and gonorrhea." She warned the Calgary school district against promoting homosexual behavior among school children because of the serious health risks.

In August, 1984, just three years after AIDS was diagnosed as a public health threat to homosexuals, columnist Patrick Buchanan and researcher Dr. J. Gordon Muir published an in-depth look at the "Gay" lifestyle and the diseases associated with it in the *American Spectator.* Writing in "Gay Times and Gay Diseases," the authors described a series of serious diseases comprising the "Gay Bowel Syndrome."

Those viruses, parasites, and bacteria resulting from homosexual sexual practices include: Amebiasis, a parasitic colon disease which causes dysentery and liver abscesses; Giardiasis, parasite that causes diarrhea; Shigellosis, another bowel disease causing dysentery; and Hepatitis A, a viral liver disease spread by fecal contamination.

According to Buchanan and Muir, San Francisco saw a four-to-ten-fold increase in gay bowel diseases beginning in 1977. As long ago as 1988, San Francisco had a venereal disease infection rate 22 times the national average. . . .

Oral and Anal Sex Can Transmit HIV

In August, 2001, researchers at the University of California released the results of a preliminary study of the risk of getting HIV from oral sex. They claimed that homosexuals are at a zero to 2% risk of getting HIV from oral sex. But a study released earlier in 2001 indicated that oral sex is implicated in at least 8% of HIV infections. This earlier study was published in February by the CDC and the University of California at San Francisco.

In the U.S., anal intercourse continues to be the primary transmission route of HIV infection for homosexuals. The CDC says there are

Fire Island Pines, New York, a popular resort at the center of the gay revolution in the 1970s, was forever changed by AIDS.

40,000 new infections each year and the rate of infection is climbing because many younger homosexuals are engaging in risky behaviors. Many have become complacent about the epidemic because of new drugs that control the progression of the disease. As a result, homosexuals are staying alive longer and infecting more individuals. As of 1998, 54% of all HIV infections were homosexuals. An estimated 1 million Americans have been infected with HIV since it was first discovered in the early 1980s. Worldwide, 21 million people have died; 450,000 Americans have died so far from HIV-related diseases.

Homosexuals Have a High Rate of STDs

A 1999 study published in the *American Journal of Public Health* indicated that homosexuals are five times as likely to have Hepatitis B as their heterosexual counterparts. A 1999 study in *Sexually Transmitted Diseases* indicated that 25% of homosexuals have rectal Gonorrhea, and Gonorrhea of the throat is prevalent because of oral sex practices. The book *The Ins and Outs of Gay Sex: A Medical Handbook for Men* states that more than 50% of homosexual males have the Human Papilloma Virus. Homosexuals are acquiring Syphilis in record numbers. The CDC released two reports on Syphilis in February, 2001. One report said that Syphilis rates had declined by 22% in the U.S. since 1997. The second indicated that Syphilis rates among homosexuals in Southern California had risen from 26% to 51% in one year. The report also noted that in Southern California alone, 60% of Syphilis-infected homosexuals were also HIV positive. . . .

Homosexual Behavior Must Be Discouraged

Dr. Diggs notes, *"A compassionate response to requests for social approval and recognition of GLB [gay, lesbian, bisexual] relationships is not to assure gays and lesbians that homosexual relationships are just like heterosexual ones, but to point out the health risks of gay sex and promiscuity. Approving same-sex relationships is detrimental to employers, employees, and society in general."*

Homosexual sex leads to serious venereal diseases, anal and oral cancer, and death from HIV infection. This behavior must be discouraged—not promoted as an alternative lifestyle. SODOMY KILLS.

EVALUATING THE AUTHORS' ARGUMENTS:

The Traditional Values Coalition accuses the homosexual population of fueling the AIDS and STD epidemic. How do you think Matthew S. Bajko, author of the following viewpoint, would respond to this accusation? Give a detailed answer that incorporates evidence from the viewpoints.

Gay Communities Have Been Effective at Reducing the Spread of STDs

Matthew S. Bajko

"'Gay men are the reason why the rates [of STDs] are coming down.'"

In the following viewpoint Matthew S. Bajko argues that homosexual behavior does not play a role in the spread of STDs. In fact, rates of some STDs in the gay community have declined by as much as 30 percent. Bajko explains that gay men are increasingly aware of the dangers inherent in certain sexual practices. As a result, more and more are taking precautions to prevent the transmission of STDs between sexual partners. Helping them do so is the development of new STD screening methods, the introduction of health-care campaigns that increase knowledge and awareness about STDs, and the creation of specialized STD treatment centers. Bajko concludes by saying that homosexual men are taking an active role in reducing the spread of STDs in their communities.

Matthew S. Bajko is an assistant editor for the *Bay Area Reporter*, San Francisco's oldest and largest local newspaper of record serving the lesbian, gay, bisexual, and transgender communities.

AS YOU READ, CONSIDER THE FOLLOWING QUESTIONS:
1. In what year does the author say that cases of STDs in the gay population began to decline?
2. What six factors does the author say contributed to the drop of STDs in the gay community?
3. How does the Internet help gay men practice safe sex, according to the author?

D uring the first six months of 2005 the number of syphilis cases in San Francisco dropped by 27 percent. It is the first time in seven years that the city has seen a decline in the sexually transmitted disease known to increase a person's chances of contracting HIV.

STDs Are Declining in the Gay Male Population

Beginning in 1998 San Francisco saw its syphilis cases double from year to year, alarming health officials who feared HIV rates would follow suit, especially in gay men who accounted for most of the STD cases. Instead, HIV rates are on the decline this year [2005] for the first time in years and never skyrocketed in tandem with the syphilis numbers.

In addition to the drop in syphilis, the city has also seen stabilization this year—and the first signs of a decline—in its number of male rectal chlamydia and male rectal gonorrhea cases. In years past the city had seen cases of both STDs rise.

"Overall, the state of male sexual health, particularly gay male health, in the city looks better," said Dr. Jeffrey Klausner, director of the health department's STD prevention and control branch.

"It is a pretty good summer for San Francisco," Charlotte Kent, chief of the epidemiology unit for the San Francisco STD control program, said of the turnaround in both HIV rates and STDs.

Steve Gibson, director of Magnet, the 2-year-old gay men's health center in the Castro [a San Francisco neighborhood], credited gay men for making the decline in STD cases possible.

"Gay men are the reason why the rates are coming down. That is very good news and should be celebrated," said Gibson.

STD Prevention Is Working

Based on data contained in the city's July 22 [2005] monthly STD report, the number of cases of adult syphilis through June numbered 251 this year compared to 346 during the first six months of 2004. Despite a sharp rise in syphilis cases during the month of June, health officials are hopeful the downward trend will continue through December and into 2006.

"I think it is a real decrease and represents effective syphilis prevention," said Klausner. "We were seeing a doubling of the number of cases every year from 1998. That doubling stopped in 2003. In 2004 it was still above 2003 but much less so. This is the first year, in 2005, we have seen a significant decline."

While gonorrhea cases overall are slightly higher this year—1,153 compared to 1,059 in June of 2004—the number of male rectal gonorrhea cases are practically the same. The city counted 212 cases so far

Free Rapid Testing sites, such as in Los Angeles, California, may be partially credited for recent declines in HIV and other STDs in gay communities.

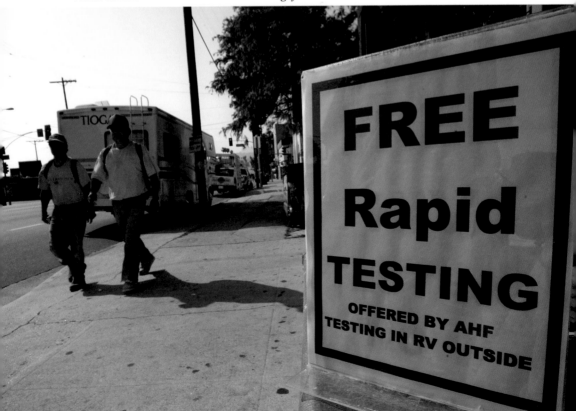

this year compared to 214 last year at this time. In regard to chlamydia, the cases are showing signs of dropping, with the total number of chlamydia this year at 1,793 compared to 1,885 last year. As for male rectal chlamydia the city saw 214 cases so far this year compared to 235 by June 2004.

"[With] the rectal chlamydia and rectal gonorrhea infections we spent less effort on testing people and on partner management, but the fact they are flat or potentially declining is a big change from years past. Every other year we saw steady increases; this is the first year we see a potential flattening," said Klausner.

Testing Reduces STDs

Since 2000 the city began doing rectal screening for both STDs, and with the opening of Magnet and extending rectal screening to other sites, Klausner said those efforts are beginning to pay off.

"Rectal screening is important because rectal infections like gonorrhea and chlamydia increase an individual's risk of getting infected with HIV at least five times. It has a very powerful effect on a person becoming infected," said Klausner. "Before 2000 there wasn't really routine screening or testing of people who have no symptoms. We didn't have Magnet, this huge new clinical service and screening center in the heart of the Castro. We didn't have screening among HIV-positive people and HIV care sites, which we now have, not completely but mostly."

Raising Awareness Reduces STDs

Klausner credited several factors for the recent declines in STDs, including more people getting tested for syphilis; the launch of Magnet; increased knowledge among medical care providers about the need to screen their patients for STDs; increased efforts people have made to tell their partners to get tested and treated; and the introduction of such healthcare campaigns as the Healthy Penis ads that educated gay men on the need to get tested for syphilis; and Inspot, an online system for people to notify their partners they may be infected with an STD.

"Our public health strategy and the community's acceptance and participation in that strategy have shown to be pretty effective at bringing down the numbers of syphilis cases," he said.

Gibson said Magnet's impact on gay men's health has been two-fold: first is the fact it is open on weekends and evenings so men who cannot access City Clinic [a clinic that diagnoses and treats STDs] during the day have a place to go, and second is its goal of extending the focus on the health of gay men beyond HIV.

"We are re-educating people on the need to get screened for other STDs on a regular basis," he said. "The Healthy Penis campaign did a great job of raising awareness about syphilis in the community. Syphilis sores don't just appear on the penis, you can have an ulcer in your throat or rectum and not know it. The ulcer is not painful, it is painless and it doesn't hurt."

Gibson said that currently, Magnet and City Clinic are the only two places that do both rectal and pharyngeal (throat) testing for gonorrhea and chlamydia. The tests are key, he said, because most of the cases of the two STDs in Magnet's patients are not found in the penis.

"Most of the cases we are finding are rectal and pharyngeal at Magnet, not urethral," said Gibson. . . .

> **FAST FACT**
>
> A study published in the *Journal of Acquired Immune Deficiency Syndromes* reports that the number of gay men who engage in unprotected sex decreases by 26 percent if they receive information on HIV prevention.

Education Reduces STDs

The STD branch is retiring its Healthy Penis ads and will be launching a new campaign this month to educate gay men about the various STDs and what impacts they have on one's health. The Healthy Penis characters will remain a fixture at community events, such as the Folsom and Castro street fairs as well as bars and clubs.

"The new campaign is about knowledge and increasing people's knowledge about STD rates," said Klausner, adding the ads will talk about how crystal [meth drug] use impacts STDs, how a person's number of sexual partners increases the risk for STDs, and what risks are linked to different sexual behaviors.

Klausner also hopes to expand his department's online testing site to also include other STDs. The program currently is focused on

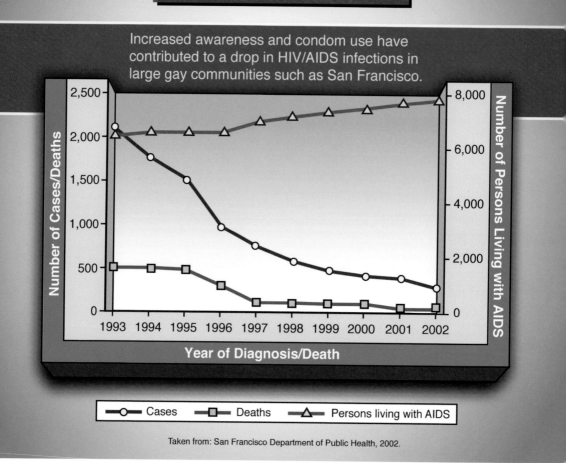

HIV/AIDS Is Declining in the Gay Community

Increased awareness and condom use have contributed to a drop in HIV/AIDS infections in large gay communities such as San Francisco.

Year of Diagnosis/Death

Legend: —○— Cases —□— Deaths —△— Persons living with AIDS

Taken from: San Francisco Department of Public Health, 2002.

getting gay men to test for syphilis and has gone from an average of two users per week to five.

"People are more comfortable with it and more confident with it. It is the only public health STD testing site online in the country," he said. "Right now it is only for syphilis but we do have plans if we get more resources to expand it for other STD and other populations."

The Internet Helps Gay Men Practice Safe Sex

In 1999, Klausner was one of the first public health of officials to raise concerns about the Internet's role in spreading STDs. Since then numerous agencies across the country have used online gay chat and hookup sites to expand their outreach to gay men, and a recent study found the Internet may now be helping gay men practice safer sex.

Today [2005], Klausner said the Internet has become a space where people are more comfortable disclosing their HIV status and hookup sites . . . support disclosure and discourage methamphetamine use, which health officials across the country are now targeting as a leading cause in HIV and STD transmission. This year, Klausner has tried to get www.Craigslist.org, a popular hookup site, to include a separate men seeking men page for positive men.

"I think it is under strong consideration," said Klausner, who first approached the site in May. "I don't understand what technical or other barriers there might be toward implementation. They told me it may occur and I am still waiting to see what happens.". . .

It Is Possible to Further Reduce STDs

While he would like to see a return of only 10 syphilis cases per year, Klausner said more realistically he hopes to bring the number of cases to fewer than 100 per year.

"I am not sure we will ever get back to 10 cases [like] in 1998. I would like to get back to 10 cases because that suggested no regular transmission. However, I am not sure we will ever be able to do that," said Klausner. Though he added that, "The other big factor is meth. If we can get a handle on crystal meth use, a drug fueling the continued drive of STDs and HIV, it may be a possibility."

EVALUATING THE AUTHOR'S ARGUMENTS:

Matthew S. Bajko quotes from several sources to support the points he makes in his essay. Make a list of everyone he quotes, including their credentials and the nature of their comments. Then analyze his sources—are they credible? Are they well qualified to speak on the subject?

Substance Abuse Contributes to the Spread of STDs

National Survey on Drug Use and Health

"The likelihood of having an STD in the past year was related to the frequency of alcohol use during the past month."

In the following viewpoint the National Survey on Drug Use and Health (NSDUH) argues that alcohol and drugs contribute to the spread of STDs. People who use alcohol and drugs are more likely to contract an STD than those who abstain from these substances, according to the NSDUH. This is because alcohol and drugs impair a person's decision-making abilities, making them less likely to discuss their sexual history prior to sex or use protection during sex. The author concludes that curbing the spread of STDs will involve campaigns that target substance use.

The National Survey on Drug Use and Health is published periodically by the U.S. government's Office of Applied Studies, Substance Abuse and Mental Health Services Administration, which provides the latest data about alcohol and drug abuse.

National Survey on Drug Use and Health, "Sexually Transmitted Diseases and Substance Use," *National Survey on Drug Use and Health*, March 30, 2007.

AS YOU READ, CONSIDER THE FOLLOWING QUESTIONS:
1. According to the author, there were how many new cases of chlamydia, gonnorhea, herpes, and syphilis in the United States in 2005?
2. Heavy drinkers made up what percent of the population with STDs, according to the author?
3. How do STD rates compare in eighteen-year-olds to twenty-five-year-olds who use alcohol and illicit drugs with those who use neither alcohol nor drugs, according to the author?

S exually transmitted diseases (STDs) are infections transmitted mainly through sexual activity, although some STDs can be transmitted by sharing drug injection equipment. In the United States in 2005, there were 976,445 new cases of chlamydia, 339,593 new cases of gonorrhea, 266,000 new cases of herpes, and 8,724 new cases of syphilis. Sexually active adolescents and young adults may be at higher risk of acquiring STDs than older adults. Recent estimates suggest that persons aged 15 to 24 represent about 25 percent of all persons who were ever sexually active, but nearly half of all new STD cases. In addition, research has documented the association between substance use and STDs.

Determining STD History

The National Survey on Drug Use and Health (NSDUH) asks questions to examine health conditions, including STDs. Respondents are provided with a list of health conditions and are asked to indicate whether they have ever been told by a doctor or other medical professional that they had each of these conditions. Individuals who report having ever been told they had any of these conditions then are asked to indicate whether they had been told by a doctor or other medical professional that they had each of the conditions in the past year. One of the conditions asked about is STDs, such as chlamydia, gonorrhea, herpes, or syphilis.

Defining Alcohol and Drug Use

NSDUH also asks persons age 12 or older to report on their use of alcohol and illicit drugs in the past month. Those who report having

Illegal drug use has been closely tied to the spread of STDs.

used alcohol are asked about binge and heavy use. *Binge Alcohol use* is defined as drinking five or more drinks on the same occasion (i.e., at the same time or within a couple of hours of each other) on at least 1 day in the past 30 days. *Heavy Alcohol use* is defined as drinking five or more drinks on the same occasion on each of 5 or more days in the past 30 days; all heavy alcohol users are also binge alcohol users. *Illicit drugs* refer to marijuana/hashish, cocaine (including crack), inhalants, hallucinogens, heroin, or prescription-type drugs used nonmedically.

This report examines STDs among the civilian, noninstitutional-ized U.S. population aged 12 or older, with a focus on young adults aged 18 to 25. In addition, rates of past year STDs are presented by level of past month alcohol use and combination of past month alcohol and illicit drug use among young adults aged 18 to 25. Past month, rather than past year, substance use is presented because most young adults have had at least one drink of alcohol in the past year, thus making past month use a better indicator of recent drinking behavior. All findings presented in this report are based on 2005 NSDUH data.

Who Has STDs?

In 2005, 0.8 percent of persons aged 12 or older (2.0 million persons) had an STD in the past year (i.e., the year prior to the survey). Persons aged 18 to 25 were more likely to have had an STD than were persons in any other age group. Females aged 12 or older were more likely to have had a past year STD than were their male counterparts (1.2 vs. 0.5 percent). Blacks were more likely to have had a past year STD than were Hispanics, whites, Native Hawaiians or Other Pacific Islanders, Asians, and persons of two or more races (1.7 vs. 0.9, 0.7, 0.2, 0.2, and 0.3 percent, respectively).

> **FAST FACT**
>
> The Do It Now Foundation reports that 19 percent of intravenous heroin users are infected with the AIDS virus, and 35 percent of intravenous cocaine users are infected with the AIDS virus.

In 2005, 2.1 percent of young adults aged 18 to 25 had a past year STD. Females aged 18 to 25 were 4 times as likely to have had a past year STD as their male counterparts (3.4 vs. 0.8 percent). Black young adults were more likely to have had a past year STD than were white, Hispanic, and Asian young adults, as well as young adults of two or more races.

A Higher Rate of Substance Use Equals More STDs

The likelihood of having an STD in the past year was related to the frequency of alcohol use during the past month. Among young adults aged 18 to 25, 1.4 percent of those who did not drink alcohol in the past month had a past year STD compared with 2.5 percent of those

Having an STD in the past year was more common among persons aged eighteen to twenty-five who used both alcohol and an illicit drug in the past month than those who used neither alcohol nor an illicit drug.

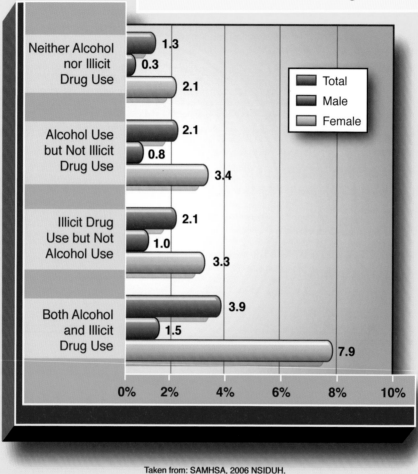

Taken from: SAMHSA, 2006 NSIDUH.

who drank but did not binge on alcohol in the past month, 2.4 percent of those who engaged in past month binge alcohol use but not heavy use, and 3.1 percent of past month heavy alcohol users. Similar patterns were found for males and females.

Having an STD in the past year was more common among persons aged 18 to 25 who used both alcohol and an illicit drug in the past month (3.9 percent) than those who used neither alcohol nor an illicit drug (1.3 percent), those who used alcohol but no illicit drugs (2.1 percent), and those who used all illicit drug but not alcohol (2.1 percent). Similar patterns were found for both males and females.

EVALUATING THE AUTHOR'S ARGUMENTS:

In the viewpoint you just read, the National Survey on Drug Use and Health (NSDUH) uses statistics to make the argument that STDs are more common in people who are heavy users of alcohol and illicit drugs than those who abstain from substance use. The NSDUH does not, however, use any quotations to support its point. If you were to rewrite this article and insert quotations, what authorities might you quote? Where would you place these quotes to bolster the points the NSDUH makes?

Lack of Education Among Senior Citizens Contributes to the Spread of STDs

Liz Langley

"Sixteen percent of newly reported HIV cases in 2005 were in people over 50."

In the following viewpoint, Liz Langley argues that a lack of education is to blame for the spread of STDs among senior citizens. There is a widespread belief that seniors are not sexually active—but, according to the author, as seniors live longer, more active lives, they are sexually active in a way Americans their age have never been before. However, seniors were born at a time when sex was not openly discussed, and education about STDs was unheard-of. Many, therefore, are unfamiliar with safe-sex practices or believe myths about STDs, such as they are too old to catch them. This has led to the rise of STDs in senior citizens

Liz Langley, "Sex and the Single Septuagenarian," Salon.com, December 4, 2006. Copyright © 2006 Salon. com. This article first appeared in Salon.com, at http://www.salon.com. An online version remains in the Salon archives. Reprinted with permission.

in recent years. The author concludes that in order to reduce the spread of STDs, health-care professionals must educate older people about STDs and how they can be avoided.

Liz Langley is a writer and pop-culture columnist for Florida's *Orlando Sentinel.*

AS YOU READ, CONSIDER THE FOLLOWING QUESTIONS:
1. What is the primary way in which seniors contract the HIV virus, according to the author?
2. What does the author mean when she says that seniors practice a "willful naiveté" when it comes to their own sexuality?
3. According to the author, why don't some seniors insist on wearing condoms during sex?

A few years ago [2001] there was a popular Pepsi commercial featuring presidential candidate and Viagra spokesman Bob Dole watching Britney Spears dance on TV. . . . This three-alarm image of the senator erect is uncomfortable on a lot of levels, but the most obvious is that people aren't used to thinking of seniors in a sexual way and aren't in a rush to start. We love to see Grandma and Grandpa running marathons, volunteering and taking tap class. But imagining them doing the mattress mambo is another story.

HIV Is on the Rise Among Seniors

Senior sexuality is certainly important in Florida, the oldest state in the country, and where, according to the U.S. Census Bureau, 17 percent of the population was 65 or over as of July 1, 2005. And those seniors aren't just sitting home playing bridge: In "Sexuality at Midlife and Beyond," a 2004 update to a 1999 AARP [a nonprofit organization for people age fifty and older] survey, more than half of respondents, aged 45 and up, cited sexual activity as a critical part of good relationships and as an important factor in quality of life. Eighty-four percent disagreed or strongly disagreed that "Sex is only for young people" and reported having intimate experiences once a week, ranging from kissing to intercourse. . . .

Of course, lives—and libidos—don't end at 50. But a growing concern is that the same parents and grandparents who once scolded their kids for playing outside without coats may not always be covering up where it counts beneath the sheets. According to Tom Liberti, chief of the Bureau of HIV/AIDS for the Florida Department of Heath [DOH] 16 percent of newly reported HIV cases in 2005 were in people over 50. . . .

Viagra and other erectile dysfunction drugs have enabled seniors to have active sex lives longer into their golden years, but those same seniors are typically not targeted with information about safety. "People don't want to think about it," says Jim Campbell, president of the National Association on HIV Over Fifty. It's an attitude he likens to "Everyone else's kid is having sex except mine." Campbell's group recently helped one nursing home establish a room for conjugal visits that couples can reserve like a hotel room. He doesn't want to say which nursing home, though, because talk of sexual matters tends to cause such consternation.

The Senior HIV Intervention Project, held in Florida, provides an opportunity for an outreach coordinator to demonstrate with his fingers how to correctly use a condom. SHIP educates seniors in safer sex practices.

"One of our counselors has a 100-year-old man with HIV," says Jolene Mullins, an early intervention consultant with the Broward County Health Department's Senior HIV Intervention Project [SHIP]. "He's newly diagnosed and how he got it we'll probably never know," though she does say sexual contact is the prime transmission method of the virus in the older population, along with some needle sharing. But consider: Even if he had been infected 25 years ago, it still would have been at age 75.

Seniors Don't Worry About STDs—but They Should

Hang on to that thought and now remember how resistant older people can be to new things. I once asked my own mother why she didn't use the microwave and she said, defiantly, "Because I'm too old." If seniors are slow to adapt to cellphones, how about using condoms? In their day they were strictly for birth control—perhaps the one health concern that seniors, luxuriously, don't have to worry about.

FAST FACT

According to an article published in *U.S. Pharmacist*, more than half of Americans age sixty years and older engage in sexual activity at least once per month.

"I never heard the word 'condom' till I don't know when. We whispered the word 'rubber,'" says Jane Fowler, 71. Even now, she jokingly rushes over the word in a phone interview from her Kansas City home. Jane has a sparkling laugh and the sweetest, most Marion Cunningham [character from the 1970s sitcom *Happy Days*] voice I've ever heard. She was diagnosed with HIV at the age of 55 and eventually co-founded the National Association on HIV Over Fifty, is co-founder and director of HIV Wisdom for Older Women, and works as an HIV/AIDS educator, speaking to groups all across the country.

In 1991 Fowler got a letter from an insurance company she'd applied to for coverage and was shocked to find she had been denied. "My blood had disclosed a significant abnormality," she says, though the letter didn't say what it was. She remembered someone had come by and stuck her finger. "He left with my application and my deposit and my blood and I didn't think any more about it, especially the blood, until I got this letter."

Using datebook diaries that go back to 1958, Fowler was able to trace not just the approximate time she was infected, but the day. After 23 years of marriage, she had unwillingly been divorced, and after awhile she started dating. "I had a few intimacies," she said. "[I wasn't] out there sleeping around . . . I didn't fit the stereotype," Fowler explains, and so wasn't the kind of person anyone would figure to test. The man she was seeing when she was infected was someone she had known for a long time. "He is not alive today," she says.

Some Seniors Practice a "Willful Naiveté"

It makes Fowler cringe when she hears about seniors who practice what she sees as a kind of willful naiveté. She picks a few names "out of the '30s" to illustrate her point. "So, you've got Betty and she's announced that she started dating Jack and she's so comfortable because she's known him for so long. She knew Jack when he was married to Mary. Then Mary died. Betty does not know what Jack was doing or what Mary was doing. You don't know what's going on in somebody's bedroom, or outside of it. I found that out myself."

People tell her, "I'm so thankful that I'm with Herb because I just never have anything to worry about." Fowler laughs. "And you think, 'OK, Marge, OK.'" Still, she says, "It's hard to stand up in front of women and suggest to them that their partner, significant other, whatever, might be having experiences outside this primary relationship."

Jolene Mullins, of the Broward County Health Department, says another concern is senior men who are gay or bisexual and may not have been able to be open about their sexuality in the past—and might not think of HIV as affecting their generation. "I can't tell you how many seniors say, 'This is not my problem,'" Mullins says. "[They ask,] 'Why are you even talking to us?'"

Healthcare Providers Should Question Seniors About Sex

A big part of that attitude relates to America's timidity in talking about sex, in Fowler's opinion. Older people are especially reluctant to do so—and often their healthcare providers don't ask. Doctors see

STDs 101

Lack of education about STDs and how they are transmitted is one reason they continue to spread. The following chart explains the most common STDs.

STD Type of Infection Location in Body	Symptoms	Prognosis and Treatment
(HPV) Human Papillomavirus Viral Located in genital skin (penis, scrotum, labia, vagina, cervix, anus)	Usually no symptoms Symptoms may include genital warts Transmission: genital skin to skin contact (vaginal, anal, oral sex, and outercourse)	Can cause cancer of the cervix, labia, anus, and penis 5,500,000 new cases per year Test: pelvic exam/pap smear Treatment: no cure. Warts are treated with chemicals, freezing, burning, or surgical removal.
(HSV2) Herpes Simplex virus Viral Located in genital area and mouth/lips (virus lives in nerves in these areas)	Usually no symptoms Symptoms may include painful blisters/sores on genital area Transmission: genital skin to skin contact (vaginal, anal, oral sex, and outercourse)	Infected for life 1,000,000 new cases per year Test: pelvic exam, culture of blisters or sores, possible blood tests Treatment: Medication may help treat sores and blisters and decrease number of outbreaks.
(HBV) Hepatitis B Virus (HCV) Hepatitis C Virus Viral Located in blood, saliva, semen, and vaginal fluid	Sometimes no symptoms Symptoms: jaundice (yellow skin or eyes), fatigue, abdominal pain, nausea, vomiting, loss of appetite Transmission: sex (vaginal, anal), I.V. drug use, contact with blood, and from mother to baby during birth	Infected for life and may cause liver failure, liver cancer, and death HBV–80,000 new cases per year HCV–40,000 new cases per year Test: blood tests Treatment: HBV–No cure, but medications can help control disease. HCV–Medications can get rid of this virus.
(HIV/AIDS) Human Immunodeficiency Virus/Acquired Immunodeficiency Syndrome Viral Located in blood, semen, vaginal fluid, and breast milk	Usually no symptoms Symptoms may include fatigue, fever, diarrhea, and other flulike symptoms Transmission: sexual activity (vaginal, anal, and oral sex); I.V. drug use; and from mother to baby during pregnancy, birth, or breast-feeding	Infected for life; immune system breaks down, leading to serious infections or cancers, often resulting in death 65,000 new cases per year Test: blood antibody screening test, DNA test, or viral titer Treatment: No cure; medications are available to slow progression of the disease.
Chlamydia Gonorrhea Bacterial infection Located in the vagina and cervix of women and urine canal in women and men; can be present in the throat (oral sex) or anus (anal sex)	Usually no symptoms Symptoms: vaginal discharge, abdominal pain, painful urination, and penile discharge Transmission: sexual activity (vaginal, anal, and oral sex)	Curable, but if left untreated can cause pelvic inflammatory disease in females leading to infertility, tubal pregnancies, and chronic pelvic pain Chlamydia–3 million new cases per year Gonorrhea–650,000 new cases per year Test: DNA test, urine test, or culture test from infected area (cervic, urethra, anus, or throat) Treatment: antibiotics by mouth or injections
Syphilis Bacterial infection Located on the mouth or genital area	Symptoms in include painless sores on the genital area, mouth, or lips; rash on hands/feet and other areas of the body; paralysis; numbness; blindness; and dementia Transmission: skin to skin contact (vaginal, anal, and oral sex)	Curable, but if left untreated can spread to the brain, heart, spinal cord, eyes, and other ares, causing damage; can cause brain damage and abnormalities in childbirth 70,000 new cases per year Test: blood test or examination of sores Treatment: antibiotics by injection
Trichomoniasis Protozoa Located in the vagina in women and urethra in men and women	Usually no symptoms Symptoms: women have frothy, yellow/green vaginal discharge with a strong odor Transmission: sexual activity (vaginal and anal sex)	Curable, but if left untreated it can cause an increased risk for acquiring HIV and may cause premature delivery in pregnant women Test: pelvic exam and laboratory tests on the vaginal or urethral fluid Treatment: antibiotics by mouth

someone who looks like their grandmother and think, "I'm not going to ask this person about sex!"

Tom Liberti, of the Florida Department of Health, says he's spoken to med students at Florida State University's School of Medicine about that very issue. "If a 60- or 70-year-old presents at a doctor's office with medical symptoms like losing weight . . . the doctor isn't necessarily going to think of HIV," but the virus doesn't discriminate. Jane Fowler offers doctors another way of looking at it: "An older person, in the confines of a provider's office, might even enjoy bragging a little bit."

Though methods of diagnosis (like the 30-minute HIV test) and medication have improved considerably, testing can still be a scary experience for anyone—but especially for seniors who are uncomfortable discussing their intimate secrets. . . .

Educating Seniors About STDs Is Necessary

Tom Liberti says that when the numbers of HIV-infected seniors in Florida climbed up to 11 percent, the Department of Health started looking at ways to reach seniors, like putting more mature faces on their health posters. Schuler is a perfect example of what an asset older people can be to their own community, simply by communicating the idea that condoms aren't just for birth control anymore.

"I can tell you the attitude of the men," says one 66-year-old woman I speak to on the phone. They come from an era where they didn't use protection, and "they think, 'I'll be dead from old age before I die of AIDS.'" She protects her friends' identities and doesn't want hers used, but says some singles insist on sexual safety, and even knows one couple who broke up over the idea. "She said she wouldn't have sex without protection. He said he wouldn't have sex with protection. That was the end of that.". . .

Edid Gonzáles, outreach coordinator for Broward County's SHIP program, says most of the seniors she tries to educate and offers to test for HIV think she's giving them good information to pass on to their grandchildren. They don't get right away that it's for them. . . .

Gentle, soft-spoken Gonzáles tries to make one of these presentations every day in hopes of reaching more South Florida seniors. For those who believe "something else will kill me first," Gonzáles' colleague Jolene Mullins says, "The virus attacks the immune system and your immune system naturally breaks down with aging. If HIV is put on top of that, it naturally enhances the problems." Then there is the challenge of seniors who have other serious illnesses, like diabetes, and must battle HIV on top of them. The complex interaction of medications is just one more risk for doctors to consider.

It All Comes Down to Prevention

It all comes down to prevention. Jane Fowler has a special maxim she likes to use at her presentations that brings it all back to Bob Dole. Back when Dole was doing ads that said it took courage to talk to your doctor about erectile dysfunction, Fowler thought he should have advocated safety, too. She even offered a line: "Now, if you can get it up, cover it up."

EVALUATING THE AUTHOR'S ARGUMENTS:

This viewpoint used narrative elements to make its point that senior citizens lack education when it comes to sex and STDs. Identify these narrative elements and explain whether they helped convince you of the author's argument.

Chapter 2

How Should the Spread of STDs Be Prevented in Teenagers?

An information table displays pamphlets and condom packages to teach teenagers safe sex practices.

Virginity Pledges Can Protect Against STDs in Teenagers

Robert Rector and Kirk A. Johnson

"Adolescent virginity pledging is strongly associated with reduced STDs among young adults."

In the following viewpoint Robert Rector and Kirk A. Johnson argue that adolescents who take virginity pledges are less likely to contract STDs than teens who do not pledge. Virginity pledges are written or verbal oaths in which teens promise to abstain from sex until marriage. Abstaining from sex removes all risk of contracting an STD. In addition to being at low risk for STDs, Rector and Johnson say that those teens who pledge to abstain from sex also are less likely to experience teen pregnancy and have fewer sexual partners over the course of their lifetimes. For this reason, the authors argue that in order to prevent the spread of STDs, teens should make and keep virginity pledges.

Robert Rector is a senior research fellow in domestic policy studies, and Kirk A. Johnson is a senior policy analyst in the

Robert Rector and Kirk A. Johnson, "Virginity Pledgers Have Lower STD Rates and Engage in Fewer Risky Sexual Behaviors," *Web Memo # 762, Heritage Foundation,* June 14, 2005. Copyright © 2005 The Heritage Foundation. Reproduced by permission.

Center for Data Analysis at the Heritage Foundation, a research and educational think tank that promotes conservative public policies based on the principles of free enterprise, limited government, and traditional American values.

AS YOU READ, CONSIDER THE FOLLOWING QUESTIONS:
1. Why are virginity pledgers at a lower risk for contracting STDs than nonpledgers, according to the authors?
2. According to Rector and Johnson, adolescents who take virginity pledges are how much less likely to contract an STD than their peers who do not take pledges?
3. In addition to having fewer STDs, what other positive life outcomes do the authors say virginity pledgers experience?

For more than a decade, organizations such as True Love Waits have encouraged young people to abstain from sexual activity. As part of these programs, young people are encouraged to take a verbal or written pledge to abstain from sex until marriage.

An article by professors Peter Bearman and Hanna Bruckner in the April 2005 issue of the *Journal of Adolescent Health* strongly attacked virginity pledge programs and abstinence education in general. The article stated that youth who took virginity pledges had the same sexually transmitted disease (STD) rates as non-pledgers. It also strongly suggested that virginity pledgers were more likely to engage in unhealthy anal and oral sex. The report garnered widespread media attention across the nation. A reexamination of the data, however, reveals that Bearman and Bruckner's conclusions were inaccurate. Moreover, in crucial respects they misled the press and public.

Virginity Pledgers Are at Lower Risk for STDs

Bearman and Bruckner tested the long-term effects of virginity pledge programs, examining the health and risk behavior of young adults (with an average age 22) who had taken a virginity pledge as adolescents. Their analysis was based on the National Longitudinal Study of Adolescent Health ("Add Health"), a database funded by the federal government. We used this same database to reexamine the issues they raised.

Several discrepancies were immediately apparent. For starters, the Add Health data clearly reveal that virginity pledgers are less likely to engage in oral or anal sex when compared to non-pledgers. In addition, virginity pledgers who have become sexually active (engaged in vaginal, oral, or anal sex) are still less likely to engage in oral or anal sex when compared to sexually active non-pledgers. This lower level of risk behavior puts virginity pledgers at lower risk for sexually transmitted diseases relative to non-pledgers.

Virginity Pledges and STDs

One study found that teens who pledged to remain a virgin until marriage had a lower incidence of gonorrhea, trichomoniasis, and chlamydia than teens who did not pledge.

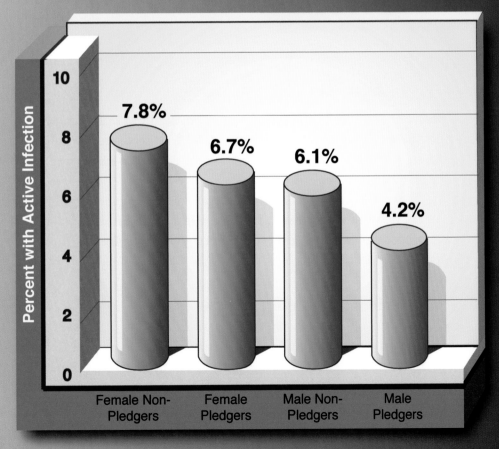

Virginity Pledgers Are Less Likely to Engage in Anal Sex

How do Bearman and Bruckner conclude the opposite? In a narrow sense, they do not. Although they strongly suggest that pledgers are more likely to engage in anal and oral sex, they never actually state that. In fact, they very carefully avoid making any clear statements about the sexual risk behaviors of pledgers and non-pledgers as a whole. Instead, they have culled through the Add Health sample looking for tiny sub-groups of pledgers with higher risk behaviors. They then describe the risk behaviors of these tiny groups and let the press infer that they are talking about pledgers in general.

The centerpiece of their argument about pledgers and heightened sexual risk activity is a small group of pledgers who engaged in anal sex without vaginal sex. This "risk group" consists of 21 persons out of a sample of 14,116. Bearman and Bruckner focus on this microscopic group while failing to inform their audience of the obvious and critical fact that pledgers as a whole are substantially less likely to engage in anal sex when compared to non-pledgers.

This tactic is akin to finding a small rocky island in the middle of the ocean, describing the island in detail without describing the surrounding ocean, and then suggesting that the ocean is dry and rocky. It is junk science.

Virginity Pledging Reduces STDs

With regard to STDs, Bearman and Bruckner actually found that adolescents who made virginity pledges were less likely to have STDs as young adults than were non-pledgers, but concluded that this difference was not statistically significant. This conclusion was based on limitations in their methodology. In fact, the same methods that they used to demonstrate that virginity pledges do not reduce STDs also demonstrate that condom use does not reduce STDs.

One problem is that Bearman and Bruckner examined only one of several STD measures available in the Add Health data file. Analysis of the remaining measures reveals that adolescent virginity pledging is strongly associated with reduced STDs among young adults. These results are statistically significant in four of the five STD measures examined and are very near significance on the fifth measure. With all the STD measures, the allegedly ineffective virginity pledge is actually a better predictor of STD reduction than is condom use. On average, individuals who took virginity pledges as adolescents were 25 percent less likely to have STDs as young adults than non-pledgers from identical socioeconomic backgrounds.

Further, Bearman and Bruckner's suggestion that virginity pledgers are ignorant about contraception is also inaccurate. Although virginity pledgers were less likely to use contraception at the very first occurrence of intercourse, differences in contraceptive use between pledgers and non-pledgers disappear quickly. In young adult years, sexually active pledgers are as likely to use contraception as non-pledgers.

Teens who make virginity pledges have a strong record of success.

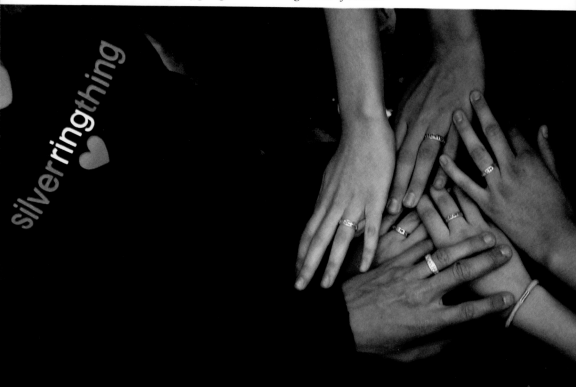

Virginity Pledgers Do Better in Life

Of course, virginity pledge programs are not omnipotent. Many years will pass between the time an adolescent takes a pledge and the time he or she reaches adulthood. These years will be full of events and forces that either reinforce or, more likely, undermine the youth's commitment to abstinence. Despite these forces, taking a virginity pledge is associated with a broad array of positive outcomes. Although most pledgers fall short of their goal of abstaining until marriage, in general, they still do a lot better in life. Compared to non-pledgers from the same social backgrounds, pledgers have far fewer sex partners. Pledgers are also less likely to engage in sex while in high school, less likely to experience teen pregnancy, less likely to have a child out-of-wedlock, less likely to have children in their teen and young adult years, and less likely to engage in non-marital sex as young adults.

Overall, virginity pledge programs have a strong record of success. They are among the few institutions in society teaching self-restraint to youth awash in a culture of narcissism and sexual permissiveness. They have been unfairly maligned by two academics who should know better.

EVALUATING THE AUTHORS' ARGUMENTS:

Robert Rector and Kirk A. Johnson argue that virginity pledgers have lower STD rates and engage in fewer risky sexual behaviors than nonpledgers. How do you think the authors of the following viewpoint, Hannah Brückner and Peter Bearman, might respond to this argument? Explain your answer using evidence from the texts.

Virginity Pledges Cannot Protect Against STDs in Teenagers

Hannah Brückner and Peter Bearman

In the following viewpoint Hannah Brückner and Peter Bearman argue that virginity pledges are not an effective tool in protecting teenagers from STDs. While many virginity pledgers promise to wait for sex until marriage, most either break their promise or engage in oral and anal sex as a substitute. But because these teens are not aware they can contract STDs through these acts, they do not take precautions to protect themselves. As a result, virginity pledgers are just as likely as nonpledgers to come into contact with an STD. Furthermore, many of these STD cases go untreated because the teens are embarrassed to admit that they have broken their pledge. Thus, these teens may unknowingly spread STDs to other adolescents. Given this, the authors recommend that virginity pledges not be used to curb the spread of STDs in teenagers.

> *"As a social policy, pledging does not appear effective in stemming STD acquisition among young adults."*

Hannah Brückner and Peter Bearman, "After the Promise: The STD Consequences of Adolescent Virginity Pledges," *Journal of Adolescent Health*, vol. 36, April 2005, pp. 271–278. Copyright © Society for Adolescent Medicine. Reproduced by permission of Elsevier, conveyed through Copyright Clearance Center, Inc.

Hannah Brückner is a professor in the Department of Sociology's Center for Research on Inequalities and the Life Course at Yale University in New Haven, Connecticut. Peter Bearman is director of the Institute for Social and Economic Research and Policy and the Lazarsfeld Center for the Social Sciences at Columbia University in New York.

AS YOU READ, CONSIDER THE FOLLOWING QUESTIONS:
1. Why might virginity pledgers have less access to information from health-care providers about sex and STDs, according to the authors?
2. What percentage of pledgers do the authors say used condoms during their first experience with oral sex?
3. According to the authors, in what ways do abstinence-only programs create barriers to knowledge about STDs?

Understanding the determinants of sexually transmitted disease (STD) acquisition among adolescents and young adults is critical to assess interventions designed to limit the spread of STDs. One set of interventions—adopted by numerous organizations and directly supported by federal policy—are programs that encourage abstinence by encouraging adolescents to make pledges to remain virgins until marriage. This article considers the relationship between adolescent virginity pledges and the sexual behavior of young adults, focusing on STD acquisition.

In 1993, "True Love Waits" initiated a movement to encourage adolescents to pledge to abstain from sex until marriage. By 1995, an estimated 2.2 million adolescents (12% of all adolescents) in the United States had taken such pledges. Earlier research demonstrated that adolescent virginity pledges were associated with a significant delay on the baseline rate for the transition to first sex. Although pledging was associated with delayed sexual initiation, the pledge effect was deeply shaped by social context, most importantly, the number of other students in the community that pledged and the social structure of the community with respect to the patterning of friendships. The pledge appears to work where public commitment to abstain from sex is encoded into shared group activities, thus enhancing identification

Virginity Pledges Do Not Protect Teens from STDs

A comprehensive study funded by the National Institutes of Health, the Centers for Disease Control and Prevention, and the National Science Foundation found that teens who take virginity pledges are just as likely to contract STDs as those who do not. Furthermore, teens who take virginity pledges are less likely to use condoms or get tested for STDs, further putting themselves at risk.

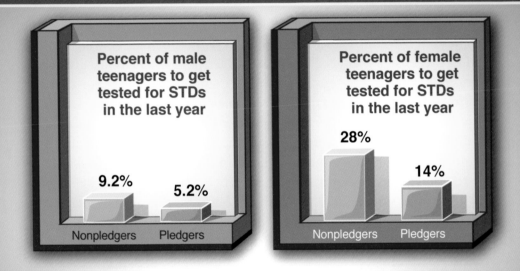

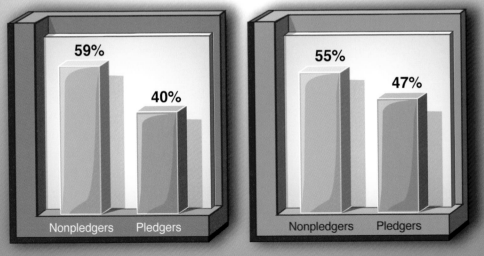

Taken from: National Longitudinal Study of Adolescent Health, 2004.

with the movement and encoding the promise to remain a virgin into the larger social fabric.

If taking a pledge indeed reduces premarital sexual activity, one might expect that pledgers are less likely to contract STDs than others because they initiate sexual activity later, have fewer sexual partners, and are more likely to have sex in the context of a marital relationship than others, all protective factors. On the other hand, pledgers may be more exposed to infection than others because they may be less likely to use condoms. We explore the sexual and health behaviors that may mediate the relationship between pledging history and later STD status. If young people take a public virginity pledge to remain virgins until marriage, having sex before marriage means that they break their pledge. Thus, sexually active pledgers have a greater incentive than nonpledgers to hide that they are having sex. Especially critical are interactions with health professionals able to provide services to those who suspect they may have an STD, pharmacists and others who provide access to condoms, contraceptive information, and STD counseling, and friends and family members who could provide relevant information about STDs, but may consider such information unnecessary. Against this background, we consider the relationship between pledging and self-reported STD-related health care utilization. . . .

Condom use at first intercourse is a powerful predictor for subsequent consistent use. As found earlier, pledgers are significantly less likely to have used a condom at first intercourse than nonpledgers. . . .

Because virginity is often culturally linked only to vaginal sex, to preserve virginity, adolescents and young adults may engage in other sexual behaviors that involve exchange of fluid and are thus salient for STD acquisition. Overall, oral sex and anal sex are prevalent behaviors in this population, most commonly in conjunction with vaginal sex. Here we consider those who have oral or anal

Abstinence-only programs that promote celibacy before marriage have been criticized for contributing to teens' misunderstandings about safe sexual choices and virginity.

sex without vaginal sex. Amongst those who have only oral sex and/or anal sex, pledgers are over-represented. Overall, about 3% of respondents reported oral sex with one or more partners but no vaginal sex. Although just over 2% of nonpledgers fall into this group, 13% of consistent pledgers and 5% of inconsistent pledgers do. Similarly, 0.7% of nonpledgers report anal but no vaginal sex, compared with 1.2% for pledgers. Although too few females report anal but no vaginal sex, for males we find a significant difference between pledgers and nonpledgers. Specifically, slightly more than 1% of male nonpledgers report anal sex but no vaginal sex, compared with almost 3% for inconsistent pledgers and 4% for consistent pledgers. For oral sex, condom use is almost completely absent—respondents reported condom use for first oral sex for only 4% of the relationships that involved oral sex. For anal sex, condom use is also lower than for vaginal sex. Condoms were used in about 30% of relationships involving anal sex when partners had anal sex for the first time. The combination of low condom use and over-representation of pledgers provides some support for the hypothesis that this behavioral pattern is associated with greater than expected STD acquisition among pledgers, although the numbers are small and provide an insufficient basis from which to make inference. . . .

Discussion

Contrary to expectations, we found no significant differences in STD infection rates between pledgers and nonpledgers, despite the fact that they transition to first sex later, have less cumulative exposure, fewer partners, and lower levels of nonmonogamous partners. Examination of the point estimates revealed small or nonexistent differences between pledgers and others, with the exception of white respondents. Advocates for abstinence-only education assert that premarital abstinence and postmarital sex are necessary and sufficient for avoiding negative consequences of sexual activity, such as STDs. This assertion collides with the realities of adolescents' and young adults' lives in several ways. First, although pledgers experience sexual debut later than others, most of them will eventually engage in premarital sex. Those who do report lower frequency of condom use at first intercourse. Those who do not are more likely to substitute oral and/or anal sex for vaginal sex.

Second, although marriage is protective against STDs, it is not perfect. Although female pledgers marry earlier, and an estimated 12% did not report any premarital sex, married pledgers test positive at the same rates as married nonpledgers. . . . As a social policy, pledging does not appear effective in stemming STD acquisition among young adults.

Furthermore, because most adolescents eventually become sexually active during their teenage years, is it really wise to ban discussion of contraception and STD protection from sex education? Although virtually all adolescents say they learned about STDs in school, other studies have shown that many adolescents underestimate their infection risk and that they have mistaken ideas about what protects them from STDs and what does not. The organizations that promote pledging and other abstinence-only programs have been hostile to programs that combine abstinence education with information about how to prevent pregnancy and STDs for sexually active adolescents. The materials distributed by "True Love Waits" and other organizations teach adolescents that the only protection from pregnancy and

STDs is abstinence. The all-or-nothing approach advocated by many abstinence-only programs may create additional barriers to knowledge and protection for adolescents. For example, the emphasis on virginity may encourage adolescents to limit their sexual activity to noncoital behaviors, which may nevertheless expose them to risks of infection. In this context, it is important to know that pledgers are less likely than nonpledgers to be tested for STDs, and to have ever seen a doctor because they are worried about an STD. If STDs were more likely to go untreated among pledgers, higher STD prevalence may result even in the presence of lower incidence rates.

Systematic and rigorous evaluation of the health impact of abstinence-only programs has rarely been undertaken. The results presented in this article show that a careful evaluation should accompany the generous federal and state funds that abstinence-only programs have enjoyed. At least for one such program, pledging, our findings suggest that a short-term evaluation of the behavioral impact of sex education programs is not sufficient to predict the longer-term health impact on STD rates.

EVALUATING THE AUTHORS' ARGUMENTS:

In this viewpoint, authors Hannah Brückner and Peter Bearman argue that teenagers who make virginity pledges are just as likely as nonpledgers to contract an STD. In the preceding viewpoint, Robert Rector and Kirk A. Johnson call Brückner and Bearman's work "junk science." What do they mean by this charge? Do you agree with their criticism? Or do you think Brückner and Bearman adequately argued their case? Explain your answer, and state whether you think virginity pledge programs can reduce the spread of STDs in teens.

Viewpoint
3

Comprehensive Sex Education Can Reduce the Spread of STDs in Teenagers

"Protecting teenagers from STDs ... requires honest science, accurate medical information and responsible educational programs."

Gambit Weekly

In the following viewpoint, the editors of *Gambit Weekly* argue that comprehensive sex education programs can reduce the spread of STDs in teenagers. These programs teach adolescents about abstinence, but they also teach about birth control and how to practice safe sex to protect against STDs. The authors argue that these programs are more effective than abstinence-only programs (which teach teenagers to avoid STDs by avoiding premarital sex altogether). It is unrealistic to think that most teens will wait until marriage to have sex, say the authors. If they are going to have sex anyway, they reason, it is better for them to be armed with accurate medical information about STDs and safe sex. The authors conclude that comprehensive sex education programs arm sexually active teens with knowledge about how to protect themselves from STDs.

Gambit Weekly is a weekly newspaper that covers politics, arts, business, and community issues in the New Orleans area.

AS YOU READ, CONSIDER THE FOLLOWING QUESTIONS:
1. What is the difference between comprehensive sex education and abstinence-only education, according to the authors?
2. What did the National Campaign to Prevent Teen Pregnancy and Advocates for Youth find about abstinence-only programs, as reported by the authors?
3. According to the authors, what is the failure rate for latex condoms when they are properly used?

Over the past decade, most public schools in Louisiana have shifted to "abstinence-only" education, which promotes abstinence until marriage and forbids discussions of condoms and birth control. At first, that might seem like a good idea. After all, what parents wouldn't want their school-age children to abstain from sex? But a growing body of research is showing that "abstinence-only" education is not only ineffective, but also, in some cases, counterproductive.

Abstinence-Only Education Is Well Funded

Statewide, only a few public school districts—including New Orleans—teach comprehensive sex education, which emphasizes abstinence but also includes messages about birth control and disease prevention. That number of districts is shrinking statewide as the amount of funding for abstinence-only education increases. In fiscal year 2005, abstinence-only programs are slated to receive $167 million in federal funding, double the amount received in fiscal year 2001. Groups that receive funding through any of three federal abstinence initiatives must comply with eight points, which specify, among other things, that "sexual activity outside marriage is likely to have harmful psychological and physical effects."

Louisiana's program—the Governor's Program on Abstinence (GPA)—is highly regarded by abstinence-only advocates nationwide. Trinidad and Tobago [a twin island republic in the Caribbean] recently adopted a version of it as well. Advocates often call GPA "the Foster plan" for former Gov. Mike Foster, whose administration oversaw the program's inception. Gov. Kathleen Blanco also is a staunch abstinence-only supporter.

Abstinence-Only Programs Are Ineffective

The Louisiana program has not been without controversy. In 2002, GPA made national headlines when the state American Civil Liberties Union (ACLU) successfully sued to bar the program's use of federal funds for "Christ-centered" skits, religious youth revivals and biblical instruction on purity. In November, the ACLU charged in a five-page complaint that the state is violating that prohibition. For instance, articles in the "library" on GPA's Web site (AbstinencEdu. com) contain assertions like this one: "The condom's biggest flaw is that those using it to prevent the conception of another human being are offending God."

Opponents of abstinence-only say that those programs allow instructors to mention birth control and condoms only in terms of failure rates. "If a student asks a teacher, a nurse, a counselor, about anything related to sex, the only acceptable response is, 'You don't have sex until you're married,'" says Tamara Kreinen, president of the New York–based group SIECUS, the Sexuality Information and Education Council of the United States.

> **FAST FACT**
>
> A survey taken by the Annenberg Public Policy Center found that 82 percent of U.S. adults support comprehensive sex education.

In December, a report released by Rep. Henry Waxman (D-Calif.) discussed studies by groups including the National Campaign to Prevent Teen Pregnancy and Advocates for Youth, which found that

High school health classes often include lectures on AIDS and sexual disease prevention.

abstinence-only programs showed some increases in positive attitudes toward abstinence but no lasting impact on behavior. Other studies have shown that while some students delay sex, most still became sexually active, and when they did, they were less likely to use contraception. In other words, abstinence-only campaigns usually fail to prevent premarital sex, but they are somewhat effective in discouraging the use of birth control.

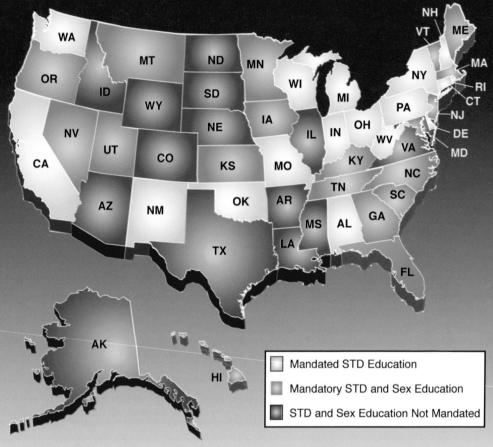

Twenty states and the District of Columbia mandate that schools teach sex education, but these programs differ in how they handle discussions of abstinence. Thirty-six states (and D.C.) require that students be taught about sexually transmitted diseases, differing in their approach on how to handle abstinence and contraceptives.

Mandated STD Education

Mandatory STD and Sex Education

STD and Sex Education Not Mandated

Taken from: "State Policies in Brief: Sex and STI/HIV Education," Guttmacher Institute, December 1, 2007.

Abstinence-Only Programs Spread Inaccurate Information

Many abstinence-only programs also promote medically inaccurate information. Waxman's report found that 80 percent of the most widely used classroom guides contained "false, misleading, or distorted information about reproductive health." Some curricula claimed that condoms fail to prevent HIV transmission as often as 31 percent of the time. If used properly, the failure rate for latex condoms is actually closer to about 2 percent, according to the government's own Centers for Disease Control and Prevention (CDC). Another curriculum contended that people can contract HIV through tears or sweat, despite the CDC's finding that "contact with saliva, tears, or sweat has never been shown to result in transmission of HIV."

Looking closer to home, we found that the Louisiana GPA promotes medical inaccuracies through its Web site, which is maintained by the Louisiana Family Forum. One GPA "expert" perpetuates a myth, contradicted by the American College of Obstetricians and Gynecologists, that there is a link between abortion and breast cancer. Several parts of the site cast doubt on condoms' scientifically proven ability to prevent the spread of sexually transmitted diseases and HIV. For example, Massachusetts-based Dr. John R. Diggs Jr. notes that "one chemist has published several compelling articles in the rubber industry journals which indicate that there are flaws in condoms big enough to allow HIV organism passage." That's a disproven and dangerous assertion to make in a state like Louisiana, where the HIV/AIDS rate is startlingly high. Another alarming passage comes from Louisiana GPA medical advisor Dr. Dee Burbank, who describes 95 percent of all sexually transmitted diseases as incurable. Most are both treatable and curable.

Comprehensive Sex Education Helps Prevent STDs in Teenagers

On the heels of Waxman's report, the American Medical Association announced that it would oppose federal funding for any programs not proven effective by independent scientific research. Senate Majority Leader Bill Frist (R-Tenn.), a physician, has said that the government should review all programs, including federally funded abstinence programs, for accuracy. Abstinence remains every parent's goal for teenage children, but the facts of life are these: studies show that about half of all high-school students are sexually active; nearly two-thirds have sex by the time they graduate. Protecting teenagers from STDs and unwanted pregnancies requires honest science, accurate medical information and responsible educational programs.

EVALUATING THE AUTHORS' ARGUMENTS:

The authors of this viewpoint argue that since teenagers are probably going to have sex before marriage, they might as well be armed with information to make their sexual encounters as safe as possible. To make their argument, the authors assume that teens will not wait until marriage to have sex. Do you think this assumption is correct? Or, is it wrong to assume that teenagers will not wait to have sex? Explain your reasoning, and then state your preference for either comprehensive sex education programs or abstinence-only programs.

Comprehensive Sex Education Cannot Reduce the Spread of STDs in Teenagers

"Comprehensive sex education is not about encouraging kids to use condoms."

Family for a Moral America

In the following viewpoint Family for a Moral America argues that comprehensive sex education programs do not reduce the prevalence of STDs in teens. Although comprehensive sex education programs tout condoms and other contraceptives as a way to avoid STDs, the reality is that contraceptives often malfunction or are used improperly. Therefore, teens should not be taught that the mere use of contraception will protect them, says the authors. In addition, there is no clinical proof that condoms stop the transmission of certain STDs such as chlamydia. The authors conclude that abstinence-only programs should replace comprehensive sex education programs because abstaining from sex is the only surefire way to avoid an STD.

Family for a Moral America is a conservative organization whose mission is to strengthen America's moral values. The following viewpoint is taken from its Web site.

AS YOU READ, CONSIDER THE FOLLOWING QUESTIONS:
1. What myth do the authors say comprehensive sex education promotes about sex?
2. According to the authors, what is the main purpose of contraceptives?
3. What do the authors claim is the best way for teenagers to avoid STDs?

Utah legislators are currently battling over sexuality education for our young people. The battle can be described as "will my child be taught abstinence until marriage," or "will they be taught comprehensive sex education?" While abstinence education is continually misrepresented by its opponents, studies show that when parents become aware of what abstinence education versus what "comprehensive" sex education really teaches, support for abstinence programs increases dramatically.

Comprehensive Sex Education Spreads Myths About Sex

[Utah senator] Scott McCoy points to a study that seemingly indicates abstinence programs are ineffective. However, the Mathematica Research study he refers to examined only four out of more than 700 Title V abstinence programs. These narrow findings represent less than 1 percent of all Title V projects across the nation. The four programs pointed to in the study were given to 11- and 12-year-olds and there was no follow up through the teen years.

The fact is, comprehensive sex education is not about encouraging kids to use condoms. Comprehensive sex education is about indoctrinating teens with the myth that having sex is about "doing what's right for you"—whenever you want, with whomever you want, and however you want. Oh, and by the way, if you don't want to get pregnant you may want to use birth control—can you pass the banana for a demo, please?

Contraception Does Not Protect from STDs

If the concern is about rising sexually transmitted disease rates, then a few relevant points need to be made: The main purpose of contraceptives is to prevent pregnancy. The main purpose of most contraceptives is NOT to prevent the spread of sexually transmitted diseases. In fact, most contraceptive methods provide absolutely NO protections against STDs. The only contraceptive methods that have been proven to provide any protection against STDs are the male condom and, to a limited degree, spermicide.

However, the risk reduction rates so oft repeated by those favoring comprehensive sex education rarely mention that those numbers are only accurate when condom use is consistent and correct 100 percent of the time. Any error, and there are lots that are made, decreases the effectiveness.

Condoms do not always prevent sexually transmitted diseases from any area not directly covered by a condom.

Condoms do not prevent the transmission of STDs from any area that is not directly covered by the condom. In addition, a recent review by the Centers for Disease Control determined that there is no clinical proof that condoms are effective in reducing the risk of chlamydia. Nor do they provide any protection against HPV or trichomoniasis. And despite all these facts, the practical reality is that men don't like condoms, and a male teen is even less likely to use one.

Here's another little secret: virtually every STD can be transmitted during vaginal, anal or oral sex. Most young people believe that if it's not vaginal intercourse, it's not sex. Therefore, even if they're engaging in oral sex with multiple partners, they don't see themselves as being sexually active. Oral sex has been found to spread syphilis, gonorrhea, HIV, HPV, genital herpes, chlamydia and possibly hepatitis C. Anywhere genital contact is involved, a person puts himself/herself at risk.

Abstinence Is the Best Protection Against STDs

Abstinence-based education is not about sticking your head in the sand—it is about encouraging our youth to make wise and healthy choices in all areas of their lives, and educating them that the surest way to avoid pregnancy and/or infection with any sexually transmitted disease is to postpone any sexual activity until marriage with an uninfected partner and remaining sexually faithful to that one partner.

> **FAST FACT**
>
> According to a poll sponsored by the Kaiser Family Foundation, National Public Radio, and the Kennedy School of Government, 7 percent of adults believe sex education should not be taught in schools.

Will they all listen? Of course not. Americans have been ignoring the Health Department for years regarding healthy eating and getting exercise, but that doesn't mean the message is flawed. It means people will sometimes make bad choices regardless of the facts and the effect on their health.

Yet no one seems to be knocking down doors on Capitol Hill complaining that our teens aren't eating healthy and ought to be taught

The Limits of Condoms

While condoms are 98 percent effective for preventing pregnancy, they are not as useful for protecting against sexually transmitted diseases.

Common STDS	Chlamydia	HSV: Herpes Simplex	Human Papillomavirus (HPV) and Genital Warts	HIV/AIDS
Can condoms help if always used (100 percent of the time and correctly)?	Condom use is associated with some decreased risk. (Risk reduction is 50 percent or less.)	Condom use is associated with some decreased risk. (Risk reduction is 50 percent or less.)	No evidence that condom use reduces risk of HPV infection. Some evidence that condoms reduce the risk of HPV-associated diseases.	Condom use decreases the risk of HIV/AIDS transmission by approximately 85 percent.

Taken from: Kate Hendricks et al., "The Attack on Abstinence Education: Fact or Fallacy?" Medical Institute for Sexual Health, May 5, 2006.

how to self-induce vomiting, have taxpayer funded access to diet pills, and gastric bypass surgery without parental consent. Rather, thinking adults acknowledge the truth behind the nutrition/exercise message and do their best to pass this information on.

The truth regarding abstinence being the safest and healthiest choice for unmarried individuals is no different. The message doesn't need to change, but the attitude toward it does.

EVALUATING THE AUTHORS' ARGUMENTS:

In this viewpoint, the authors argue that comprehensive sex education programs provide inaccurate information to teenagers about sex and do nothing to stop the spread of STDs. How do you think the authors of the preceding viewpoint, from *Gambit Weekly*, would respond to this claim? Support your answer with evidence from both essays.

Chapter 3

Should Teenagers Be Vaccinated Against STDs?

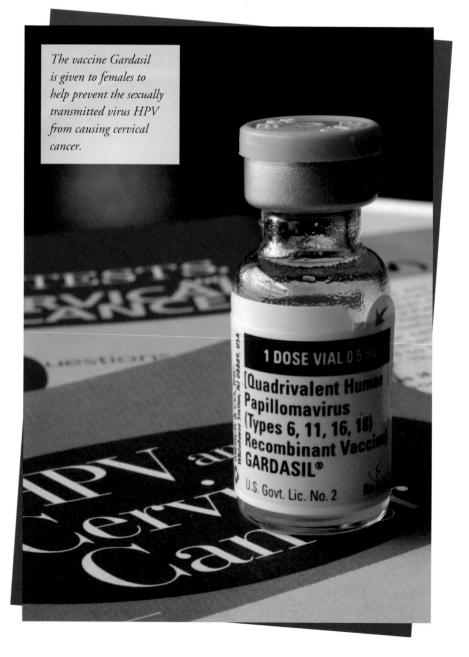

The vaccine Gardasil is given to females to help prevent the sexually transmitted virus HPV from causing cervical cancer.

Teens Should Be Vaccinated Against STDs

Carl Campanile

"Health experts say the three-dose vaccine is most effective when given to girls as young as 9."

In the following viewpoint Carl Campanile discusses that teens should be given a vaccine that will protect them against the human papillomavirus (HPV), an STD that causes genital warts and cervical cancer. Many teens become infected with HPV, but with the recent development of a drug known as Gardasil, young women can get vaccinated against HPV. If administered to teens, it could greatly reduce the occurrence of STDs. It would be ideal to administer the vaccine in schools, but fear of promiscuity among teens has put the idea on hold throughout the United States.

Carl Campanile is a journalist for the *New York Post*.

AS YOU READ, CONSIDER THE FOLLOWING QUESTIONS:
1. What is Gardasil?
2. Why would it be important to distribute Gardasil through a school-based clinic?
3. Why are some parents against having their daughters receive Gardasil?

Health officials have launched an aggressive campaign to distribute a vaccine that helps prevent cervical cancer to girls in public schools, it was revealed yesterday.

The Health Department reported that it had given out 57,810 doses of Gardasil to health providers—including to some of the 100 school health clinics that had requested the vaccine, officials said.

A teen receives her third and final application of the HPV vaccine.

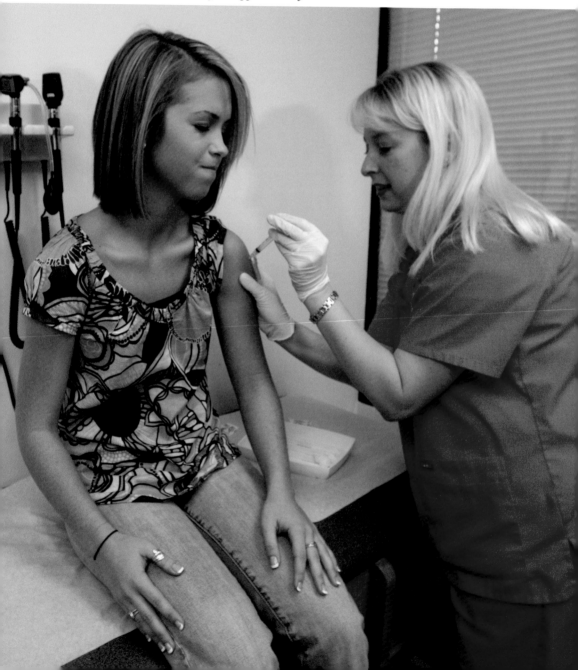

An Effective Vaccine

Gardasil helps prevent the human papillomavirus (HPV), a sexually transmitted disease that causes cervical cancer.

Health experts say the three-dose vaccine is most effective when given to girls as young as 9.

"We are already providing HPV vaccine in school-based clinics," city Deputy Health Commissioner Isaac Weisfuse said at a City Council Health Committee hearing.

Let's Protect Teenagers

Dr. Weisfuse did not specify how much of the vaccine was distributed to school clinics but said it was important to provide the vaccine in schools because teens normally don't see doctors frequently.

"Because adolescents do not utilize the primary-care system as regularly as younger children, we are identifying alternative sites to maximize access to vaccine. . . . School-based clinics and after-school programs will be recruited for the VFC [Vaccines for Children] program," he said.

The city's public hospital system also said it would also help administer the vaccine in schools.

"That's something we are exploring," said Dr. Ramanathan Raju, vice president and chief medical officer of the Health and Hospitals Corp. "We should probably look at middle schools and high schools."

The federal Vaccines for Children program provides free vaccines to girls age 9 through 18 who are on Medicaid or have inadequate insurance. State law requires that other girls get coverage through their private insurers.

Health officials were quick to note that parental consent is required to give the vaccine.

HPV Vaccine Controversy

Merck, the manufacturer of Gardasil, has backed state laws to make it easier to distribute the HPV vaccine in schools.

> **FAST FACT**
>
> The retail cost of the HPV vaccine is $360 for the three-dose series, according to the Centers for Disease Control and Prevention.

But it recently backed off its lobbying campaign following criticism that such laws would encourage promiscuity among youths.

Queens Councilwoman Helen Sears said an educational campaign would be needed for parents, some of whom may have moral objections to giving young girls a vaccine for HPV.

"I could understand why this issue has raised eyebrows," she said.

EVALUATING THE AUTHOR'S ARGUMENTS:

In this viewpoint, Carl Campanile discusses the importance of teenagers being vaccinated with Gardasil in order to prevent infection of HPV. Do you believe youths as young as nine years old should be vaccinated with Gardasil? Explain your answer with support from the text.

Teens Should Not Be Vaccinated Against STDs

"Considering how little we know [about the vaccine], are we ready to make an entire nation of preadolescent girls the subjects of a vast experiment?"

Elissa Mendenhall

In the following viewpoint Elissa Mendenhall argues that adolescent girls should not be vaccinated against human papillomavirus (HPV), a common STD. Although as many as 80 percent of women will acquire HPV by the time they are age fifty, the author argues that HPV is actually asymptomatic in most women, meaning it does not harm or cause them discomfort or pain. Since the virus is a problem in very few women, the author argues it does not make sense to vaccinate all teen girls against it. In fact, the vaccine could provide a false sense of protection and discourage women from getting annual Pap exams, the real detector of HPV and cancer. Furthermore, the author claims that the long-term effects of the vaccine are unknown. The lack of knowledge about the vaccine warrants further study before young women are given a potentially dangerous vaccine, Mendenhall concludes.

Elissa Mendenhall is a naturopathic physician who lives in Portland, Oregon. She

Elissa Mendenhall, "Guard Against Gardasil," *Mothering*, May/June 2007, pp. 44–49. Copyright © 2007 *Mothering Magazine*. Reproduced by permission of the author.

writes on health topics for various publications, including *Mothering*, from which this viewpoint was taken.

AS YOU READ, CONSIDER THE FOLLOWING QUESTIONS:
1. Of the roughly 250,000 cases of cervical cancer each year, how many women does the author say die from the disease?
2. According to the author, how might an STD vaccine deter women from getting an annual Pap exam?
3. How long does a dose of Gardasil provide protection against STDs, as reported by the author?

In September 2006, the State of Michigan approved two measures to require girls entering the sixth grade to be vaccinated with Gardasil, the new vaccine for human papillomavirus (HPV). Touted as the "anti-cancer vaccine," Gardasil is widely hailed in the public health community as a giant step toward preventing cervical cancer. After four clinical trials, the FDA approved its use in June 2006, and Gardasil is now available by prescription.

Clinical trials have found that Gardasil is nearly 100 percent effective in preventing certain strains of HPV infection—a tremendous feat in the world of vaccine research. There is no doubt that the introduction of Gardasil has dramatically altered the public-health landscape for both sexually transmitted infections and cervical cancer. But are we ready to make the leap from a handful of promising clinical trials to mandating vaccination for all preadolescent girls?

HPV Is Not Harmful to Most Women

Humans and HPV have an interesting and complex relationship. HPV is best known for causing common warts and cervical cancer, but there are more than 100 different strains of HPV. Because of the cancer link, the strains that are of the greatest medical concern are those that are sexually transmitted. These strains can cause genital warts, or can be associated with cervical and other cancers of the genital area. Approximately 13 percent of American women are infected with genital HPV. Infection with the HPV virus is an important cofactor in cervical cancer, but very few people infected with HPV will ever get cervical cancer. At least 80 percent of women will have acquired a genital HPV infection by the time they are 50 years old, and about 6.2 million American men and women get a new genital HPV infection each year, according to estimates by the Centers for Disease Control. Compare this to the national rate of cervical cancer. In 2003, the National Cancer Institute estimated the number of cases of cervical cancer at 253,781. In 2002, 4,000 women died from the disease in the US. While this is a sizable number, it represents a tiny fraction of those infected with the virus. HPV infection is asymptomatic in most people. Until recently, most cases went undetected.

With recent advances in detection of the HPV virus, it appears that the norm is more one of infection than of disease. In most cases, the virus's relationship with its host is symbiotic: It causes no harm and is not easily detected. "Although HPV is a necessary cause of cervical cancer, it is not a sufficient cause. Thus, other cofactors are necessary for progression from cervical HPV infection to cancer," states Nubia Munoz in a recent article in the medical journal *Vaccine*. Saying that HPV causes cervical cancer is similar to saying that being of African descent causes sickle-cell anemia: It is an oversimplification that fails to look at other factors. For instance, the World Health Organization notes that up to 30 percent of cervical cancer deaths in the US are attributable to smoking cigarettes. . . .

Is a Vaccine Necessary?

The FDA categorized Gardasil as a drug that has the potential to provide "significant health benefits." But exactly how big is the current risk of cervical cancer in the US? There is no doubt that, every year, the disease kills American women. However, cervical cancer is not usually a quickly progressing, invasive cancer. And it generally

> **FAST FACT**
>
> The National Vaccine Information Center reports that 15 to 20 percent of all adverse reactions to vaccines involve Gardasil.

responds well to treatment. It is also true that the vast majority of women with cervical cancer are infected with HPV. On the other hand, the vast majority of women infected with HPV never get cervical cancer.

This brings into question cause and effect. In the journal *Vaccine,* Anna-Barbara Moscicki states that, "Given the ubiquity of HPV, the most critical step in cervical carcinogenesis [cancer initiation] is not acquisition of the infection, but rather the step involving progression to clinically important lesions." In other words, it's not getting HPV that matters, it's what happens afterward. Cervical cancers diagnosed in their early stages are rarely fatal. Most fatalities are due to lack of detection and treatment.

Regular Pap Tests Prevent Cervical Cancer

The important keys to the prevention of cervical cancer are getting regular testing with annual Pap screens and modifying other risk factors. Getting early treatment is also important.

Regular Pap tests have reduced the rate of death from cervical cancer by at least 75 percent since the 1960s. Compared to screening for other types of cancer, Pap screening is considered by health-care practitioners to offer one of the best ratios of screening to actual prevention. It was no small feat for the public health community to establish annual Pap screening for women in the US but it was worth the effort. Vaccination against HPV could change all of that.

A Vaccine Might Discourage Annual Pap Screening

The way Gardasil is being hailed in the media and advertisements, it is easy to understand how a young woman vaccinated with it might think that she has been protected against cervical cancer. Merck's campaign slogan, "One Less," implies that each woman who receives a Gardasil vaccination will be one less victim of cervical cancer. However, this idea of sure protection against cervical cancer is not only untrue but dangerous. Gardasil prevents infection by only four of the more than 100 strains of the HPV virus. This is why it is thought that the vaccines will prevent, at most, only 70 percent of cervical cancers. But what if women infected with the other 30 percent of the cancer-causing strains of HPV decide to forgo their annual exams because they have been vaccinated with Gardasil and thus believe they are protected? Overall, we would see a decrease in the number of HPV infections, but a large increase in fatalities from cervical cancer. The public research has not yet been done to see if this effect would occur.

Greg Zimet, PhD, a clinical researcher at the Indiana University School of Medicine, has published several articles in medical journals

A mother voices her opposition to a measure that would require middle-school-aged girls to be vaccinated against HPV.

about Gardasil. Although in favor of the vaccine, he concedes that a reduction in the number of women getting annual Pap tests might be an "unanticipated cost" of the vaccine's approval by the FDA; he emphasizes that "this does not change the need for regular Pap testing." After 30 years of success in the public health sector with Pap tests and cervical cancer screenings, it would be a shame to backslide now.

An STD Vaccine Would Not Be Available to Everyone

Compare the statistics of cervical cancer in the US those in places where the rates of cervical cancer and death from it are still high. In Haiti, the poorest country in the Western Hemisphere, cervical cancer accounts for nearly half of cancer deaths; in the US, 2.5 percent. Regular screenings make the difference. In places such as Haiti, where most people cannot afford and/or have no access to regular screening, Gardasil may be just what the doctor ordered. However, Gardasil is an expensive vaccine, and is not marketed toward or currently available to these poorer populations; and in the US, it may actually cause more deaths from cervical cancer.

Another issue that only long-term research will resolve is how long a single vaccination with Gardasil will provide protection. So far, trials have shown that it sustains an immune response for five years, but it is still far too early to know whether immunity granted by Gardasil is lifelong or temporary. Knowing this will have a large impact on when, how, and if young women should be vaccinated.

Not Enough Information to Vaccinate

Do Gardasil's potential benefits outweigh the risks? Perhaps, but only time will tell. If it is similar to the hepatitis B vaccine introduced some years ago, it is still far too soon to know. "As shown by research on hepatitis B vaccination, many key answers only became known at least ten years after the vaccine first became available," states Eduardo Franco, of McGill University, Montreal, Canada, in *Vaccine*.

The bottom line is that we don't yet have enough information to know whether young women should be vaccinated en masse with Gardasil.

We know that it is effective in conferring immunity against HPV. What we don't know is if it is safe to use with adolescents. Nor do we know anything about its long-term safety and efficacy with any age group. Nor do we know if mass vaccinations will cause a decline or an increase in deaths from cervical cancer. Considering how little we know, are we ready to make an entire nation of preadolescent girls the subjects of a vast experiment? At $360 for the full series of three injections, it will be challenging to even find the funding for a national vaccination campaign. Gardasil is one of the highest-priced vaccines ever marketed. It is a costly risk to take.

EVALUATING THE AUTHORS' ARGUMENTS:

The author of this viewpoint, Elissa Mendenhall, is a naturopathic physician. The author of the previous viewpoint is a journalist. On what points do they disagree? Are these disagreements related to their professions? Why or why not?

STD Vaccines Should Be Mandatory for Students

> *"Making [the HPV vaccine] mandatory for public school admission is a good way to make sure this vaccine gets widespread use."*

Mindy Townsend

In the following viewpoint Mindy Townsend argues that all students should receive mandatory STD vaccinations. Human papillomavirus (HPV), the most common and prolific STD, infects more than 20 million people, including 80 percent of women. HPV is a serious disease that can cause cervical cancer in some infected women, but a new vaccine could help prevent its spread in millions of girls and women. As such, the author argues that if all schools required preteen girls to be vaccinated against STDs before being admitted, the disease might one day be eradicated. The author concludes that if there is a safe and effective STD preventative, it is in the best interest of public health to make STD vaccinations mandatory.

Mindy Townsend is a staff writer for Collegio.com, an independent Web site published by students of Pittsburgh State University in Kansas, from which this viewpoint is taken.

AS YOU READ, CONSIDER THE FOLLOWING QUESTIONS:
1. How many people does the author say are infected with HPV worldwide?
2. What percentage of genital warts cases were prevented during clinical trials of the HPV vaccine, according to the author?
3. What does the author mean by the phrase "herd community" when discussing the effectiveness of mandatory STD vaccinations?

I hate needles.

I need to muster all my courage to give blood. When I got shots as a kid, the nurses always told me to count backward from 10 and I wouldn't feel a thing.

But it wasn't the actual sting of the needle penetrating my skin that managed to scare me. It was the thought of the needle penetrating my skin. Like a small, hollow sword. No amount of counting could ever get that image out of my head.

But I guess those darn shots worked.

Now the only thing that scares me more than needles is cancer. I perpetually think I have cancer. I even went to the doctor, just to make sure . . . and the nurse actually let me see him, just to humor me.

If only there was a vaccine for cancer.

HPV Is the Most Common STD

Well, now there is. Sort of. A vaccine has been developed that can protect against the most common STD out there, human papillomavirus, or HPV.

There are more than 30 types of HPV that are sexually transmitted. According to the Centers for Disease Control [CDC] about 20 million people are infected with HPV and 50 percent of sexually active people, both men and women, will get an HPV infection during their lifetime. At least 80 percent of women will get a genital HPV infection by the time they are 50 years old.

The CDC Web site also says that there are 6.2 million new genital HPV infections in the United States every year and the *Washington Post* says that cervical cancer kills 3,700 women per year in the United States and 290,000 more across the globe.

A genital HPV infection is caused by contact between the naughty bits. Most infections have no symptoms, so it is often transmitted unknowingly. These infections can go away on their own, but the virus can also cause genital warts and cancer. In fact, the CDC says that 10 of the 30 genital HPV types can lead to the development of cervical cancer, although it is rare.

Vaccinating Against HPV

However, cervical cancer caused by HPV may soon be a thing of the past. According to the *Washington Post*, the FDA has approved an HPV vaccine that protects against infection by four strains of HPV. In fact, clinical trials prevented 100 percent of cervical cancer for women

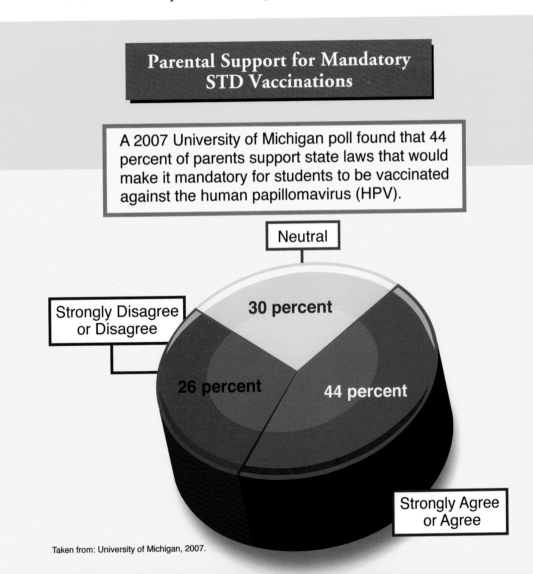

Parental Support for Mandatory STD Vaccinations

A 2007 University of Michigan poll found that 44 percent of parents support state laws that would make it mandatory for students to be vaccinated against the human papillomavirus (HPV).

Neutral

30 percent

Strongly Disagree or Disagree

26 percent

44 percent

Strongly Agree or Agree

Taken from: University of Michigan, 2007.

who have not already been infected and 99 percent of genital warts. The Merck-manufactured vaccine, called Gardasil, has been approved for use in women between the ages of 9 and 26, but the vaccine works best when given to women who have yet to become sexually active. It does not protect those who are already infected.

Gardasil is shown to be effective against two types of HPV responsible for 70 percent of cervical cancer cases, as well as two other strains that cause 90 percent of genital wart cases. And the vaccine is unique, as there is only one other vaccine that prevents cancer, and that is a vaccine against hepatitis B, which is known to cause liver cancer.

As promising as the vaccine is, there are still some unanswered questions.

The Vaccine Needs Widespread Support

The FDA says that Gardasil is safe, but it is still unknown how long the protection will last or if booster shots will be needed in the future, according to the *Washington Post*. The *Post* also points out that the three-shot series will cost $120 a shot, which could hinder widespread use. As such, it will be a challenge to provide the vaccine to the poor and disadvantaged who don't receive regular Pap smears. According to the *Washington Post*, however, Merck plans to provide the vaccine to the poor and uninsured.

The National Advisory Committee on Immunization Practices should have a decision by June 29 [2006] on whether to endorse Gardasil. And the vaccine pretty much needs that endorsement to become a standard of care.

Making the Vaccine Mandatory Protects Everyone

If there is an endorsement, it will be up to the states to decide if they want to make the vaccine mandatory to attend school, said the *Washington Post*.

Pro-abstinence conservative groups support making the vaccine available, but do not want to make it mandatory because they worry it will increase sexual activity.

I don't think anybody is disputing the potential positive impacts for women everywhere. However, vaccines are shown to be most effective in a "herd community." That is when enough people are immunized that the disease disappears. Making it mandatory for public school admission is a good way to make sure this vaccine gets widespread use.

Despite Texas governor Rick Perry's executive order requiring the HPV vaccine for middle-school girls, the House approved a bill keeping it off the list of required shots for school attendance.

A Lifesaving Vaccine

To dwell on the question of whether this is a green light for young people to have sex is ignoring the lifesaving nature of the vaccine. I also think that if young girls receive the vaccination, it will spur a much-needed dialogue with their parents about sex. There may be too much sex on TV, but how often does that actually spawn a real conversation?

But when someone is poking a small sword into my veins, I tend to ask why.

It's hard to decide what kinds of medicines should be introduced into the human body. And maybe I am overestimating the risks of getting cervical cancer caused by genital HPV.

I just know that if I had a daughter, I'd want her to have it, regardless of her fear of needles.

EVALUATING THE AUTHOR'S ARGUMENTS:

In this viewpoint Mindy Townsend argues that mandating STD vaccinations could one day eradicate deadly diseases like cervical cancer. Would you want to take a vaccine if it could potentially prevent STDs and cancer? Why or why not? Explain your answer thoroughly.

STD Vaccines Should Not Be Mandatory for Students

John R. Diggs Jr.

"The assertion that the current HPV vaccine, Gardasil, should be forced upon any [person] represents . . . an assault upon personal freedom."

In the following viewpoint John R. Diggs Jr. argues against the mandatory vaccination of students against STDs. Diggs explains that making people receive a medical procedure against their will is a violation of their privacy and an assault on their personal freedom. Furthermore, Diggs suggests there is a lack of evidence on whether the human papillomavirus (HPV) vaccine is even safe— it could have dangerous side effects that have yet to be revealed. Plus, the vaccine does not provide protection against all strains of HPV, and it does not protect adolescent boys from the disease. For Diggs, this makes it an ineffective and inequitable solution to the problem of STDs in teens. Given the large number of unknowns about the vaccine, the author vehemently argues against mandatory vaccinations.

John R. Diggs Jr. is a board-certified internal medicine specialist in South Hadley, Massachusetts. He also serves as a representative on the Select Committee of Public Health Oversight.

John R. Diggs Jr., "Testimony Against the Forced Endurance of a Medical Procedure, Human Papilloma Virus (HPV)," *Massachusetts Legislature,* July 11, 2007. Reproduced by permission of the author.

AS YOU READ, CONSIDER THE FOLLOWING QUESTIONS:
1. Of the thirty types of HPV, how many does Gardasil protect against, according to the author?
2. What percentage of the male population does the author say is susceptible to HPV infection?
3. According to the author, Gardasil has not been around long enough to document what?

I speak as a representative of the Select Committee on Public Health Oversight. I am a board-certified Internal Medicine specialist from South Hadley, Massachusetts. I graduated from Haverford College, then earned my medical degree from the State University of Buffalo School of Biomedical Sciences in 1983.

The HPV vaccine, its genesis, and its effectiveness have been of special interest to me. As a citizen of the nation and state with the longest active Constitutions, individual freedom is also a special interest.

The assertion that the current HPV vaccine, Gardasil, should be forced upon any member of the citizenry represents not only an assault upon personal freedom, but also demonstrates the power of influential lobbyists to contradict sound public health.

The idea that one can give a vaccine and prevent cancer is seductive. Perhaps it is so seductive that the idea alone demands mandatory imposition. In the case of Gardasil, eradication of cervical cancer would be a false understanding of the capability of the vaccine.

What Causes HPV?

Cervical cancer is caused by the sexual transmission of HPV. While there are 130 subtypes of HPV, only 30 cause genital disease. We classify some as 'high risk' meaning they are more likely to cause cervical cancer than the 'low risk' types. Periodically, we are forced to reclassify them when new data is generated. Each reclassification has occurred, a type we thought was low-risk is reclassified as high-risk. We have not done the reverse.

Too Many Unanswered Questions

Of the 30 types subtypes of HPV, Gardasil only protects against four; of those four, two are high-risk. At this point, we cannot state how long the protection lasts. We cannot state the effect on future fertility. The vaccine is only administered to females. It is the most expensive vaccine of the current panel of vaccines. The manufacturer has made nationwide efforts to make the vaccine mandatory. It has lobbied us physicians in such a manner that pediatricians have called parents 'irresponsible' if they refuse the vaccine for their children. More recently, the manufacturer has pulled back on its efforts because the tactics and ethical conduct were called into question.

A Vaccine Serves the Manufacturer

The motivations for rushing the vaccine to market, directly approaching legislators and even governors of a variety of states are starkly opportunistic. If the vaccine [is] mandated, the manufacturer then has a ready-made, even captive, consumer. Second, the financial responsibility of the manufacturer for adverse damage to the patient is handled differ-

Parents of girls in Vermont could "opt out" of immunizations proposed against strains of HPV on religious or moral grounds.

Legislation under Consideration for HPV Vaccination

- **Florida, Pennsylvania, Rhode Island, Connecticut**
  Require coverage of vaccine by insurers

- **California, Connecticut, Colorado, District of Columbia, Florida, Okalahoma, South Carolina, Texas, Vermont, Virginia:**
  Require vaccination for 6th graders before age 12 or 13

Adverse Reactions to Gardasil

Increasing numbers of adverse reaction reports have been filed with the Food and Drug Administration since the STD vaccine Gardasil came on the market. Adverse reactions have included fever, rash, vomiting, diarrhea, shock, swelling, fatigue, pain, headache, muscular weakness, and imbalance.

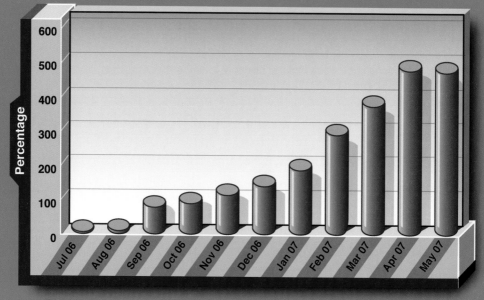

Taken from: National Vaccine Information Center, "Human Papiloma Virus Vaccine Safety," August 14, 2007.

ently; this is to the manufacturer's advantage and to the consumer's and taxpayer's disadvantage. The third point is age-old attempt to slam the competition. The big hurry is not out of compassion as one might think but is actually designed to curtail the sales of a similar vaccine in development from a competing pharmaceutical firm. If millions are vaccinated now, they will have only one vaccine from which to choose. The manufacturer hopes that by the time the second product is released from its competitor, brand loyalty will have developed.

Gardasil Will Not Protect Everbody

The populace is still highly susceptible to HPV infection and cervical cancer. First, only females are vaccinated. Even if 100% of females take a vaccine which is 100% effective, only 4 of 26 HPV subtypes will be prevented. Second, the male population will be 100% susceptible to HPV infection. While less common than cervical cancer, HPV also causes penile and anal cancer in males. Males and females will continue to be susceptible to 26 other genital HPV infections.

Forcing a Vaccine Hurts Personal Freedoms

It is not the government's job to force medical procedures on individuals unless there is a compelling interest. Genital HPV is only transmitted sexually, not through casual contact, therefore, the compelling State interest is lacking. This is in sharp contrast to polio. Polio can be spread in a common classroom environment, and it has high morbidity and mortality. The compelling interest in mandating a medical procedure in that setting is obvious. In the case of Gardasil, this argument can not be validly made.

A nation of free persons should not be forced to accept the judgment of others as regards medical procedures. If the legislature establishes this precedent, what is next—forced mammograms, forced colonoscopies?

In this Commonwealth, in this legislative body, the argument has been made and laws have been passed codifying that a woman has the right to kill her unborn child through a medical procedure, abortion, under the rubric that she controls her body. How then, if you, as a legislator find this sequence acceptable, can you even contemplate forcing another person's body to endure a medical procedure?

> **FAST FACT**
>
> An article in the *Journal of the American Medical Association* reports that only 3.4 percent of women have an infection that Gardasil protects against.

And yet, here we are today [2006], considering exactly that governmental coercive legislation.

Why a Mandatory Vaccine Is Not Effective

In summary, my testimony against the mandatory HPV vaccine is based upon the following.
- While the HPV vaccine is effective for 4 subtypes, recipients will still be subject to the other 26.

- The manufacturer gets a 'pass' on adverse effects.
- The Gardasil (vaccine) has not been in use long enough to document the prolonged effects on other body systems, including future fertility.
- Gardasil creates a false sense of security that one is protected from cervical cancer. False security is worse than truthful knowledge.
- The manufacturer has used under-handed methods to sell its product, deceptively appealing to the idea that Gardasil will stop cervical cancer. Meanwhile, the manufacturer's less transparent motivation is to capture market share.
- Up to this point, public health departments, including the Massachusetts Department of Public Health, have been remiss in educating the populace about HPV. How do we legitimately go from observably treating HPV as relatively trivial, to suddenly treating it as such a threat that ALL females of a certain age are forced to undergo this medical procedure? One cannot legitimately do so. The lack of logical sequence smacks of a hidden agenda.

Reject Mandatory Vaccinations

When agendas are hidden, they can usually be brought to light when you 'follow the money.'

I ask that you reject this legislation for mandatory HPV vaccine. The legislation assaults individual freedom, assaults the unalienable right of parents to decide how to raise their children and consent to medical interventions, and it reflects a lack of understanding of the shortcomings of this product and the nature of HPV infection.

EVALUATING THE AUTHORS' ARGUMENTS:

John R. Diggs Jr. argues there has not been enough research and testing of the HPV vaccine to prove its safety and effectiveness. How do you think the author of the preceding viewpoint, Mindy Townsend, might respond to this argument? Explain your answer using evidence from the texts.

Facts About Sexually Transmitted Diseases

Editors' note: These facts can be used in reports or papers to reinforce or add credibility when making important points or claims.

The Prevalence of Sexually Transmitted Diseases

- According to the Centers for Disease Control and Prevention (CDC), as of November 2007:
  - Approximately 1.03 million cases of chlamydia were reported to the CDC in 2006, a 5.8 percent increase over 2005.
  - In the United States, 358,366 cases of gonorrhea were reported, an increase of 5.5 percent from the previous year.
  - The rate of syphilis cases increased 13.8 percent from 2005 to a reported 9,758 cases.
  - The rate of incidences of syphilis has increased 57 percent since 2001.
  - Although young adults between the ages of fifteen and twenty-four are only one-fourth of the sexually active population, they account for nearly half of new STD cases.
  - Women between the ages of fifteen and nineteen have the highest rate of gonorrhea, 647.9 cases per one hundred thousand people.
  - Chlamydia rates increased between 2002 and 2006 by 20.6 percent among whites, 17.2 percent among African Americans, and 12.7 percent among Hispanics but declined by 5.9 percent among Asian and Pacific Islanders.
  - Approximately 47 percent of all chlamydia cases in 2006 occurred among African Americans. In addition, the rate of chlamydia among African Americans in the United States is eight times greater than that of whites.
  - In 2006 the chlamydia rate among Hispanics was three times higher than the rate among whites.
  - The rate of gonorrhea among whites is nearly two times greater than the rate for Asian/Pacific Islanders.

- Also according to the CDC:
  - One in four teenage girls in the United States has an STD.
  - Approximately 18 percent of teenage girls are infected with human papillomavirus (HPV).

- Nearly 50 percent of African American teenage girls has at least one STD.
- Approximately 3 million teenagers become infected with a sexually transmitted disease each year.
- Half of all sexually active adults acquire a genital HPV infection.
- Approximately 20 million Americans have HPV, while another 6.2 million become newly infected each year.
- There are more than one hundred strains of HPV.

- According to the United Nations Joint Programme on HIV/AIDS (UNAIDS):
  - Worldwide 33.2 million people have HIV.
  - In sub-Saharan Africa, 22.5 million people have HIV or AIDS as of 2007.
  - Some 2.5 million people with HIV are children under the age of fifteen.
  - In 2007, 2.5 million people were infected with HIV. In other words, there were 2.5 million new cases of AIDS in just that year.
  - Annual HIV infections in sub-Saharan Africa declined from 2.2 million infections in 2001 to 1.7 million in 2007.
  - Annual incidences of HIV increased in east Asia by 20 percent between 2001 and 2007.

- According to the organization AVERT, an international HIV and AIDS charity, 4.8 million people in Asia were diagnosed with AIDS by 2007.

- A Zogby poll published in August 2006 found that 37 percent of Chinese men have visited prostitutes.

- According to a report in the journal *Sexually Transmitted Infections*, almost one in every ten men has had sex with a prostitute.

- According to a report published by UNAIDS and the World Health Organization, the HIV infection rate among adults in Kenya fell from 10 percent in the late 1990s to 7 percent in 2003.

- According to the Guttmacher Institute:
  - It is reported that 40 percent of HIV cases occur in the fifteen- to twenty-four-year-old age group. Ten million people in that age group have HIV worldwide.
  - The proportion of people age fifteen and older with HIV who are women increased from 35 percent in 1985 to 48 percent in 2005.
  - Half of the people with AIDS are women of childbearing age.

The Consequences of Sexually Transmitted Diseases

- A report by UNICEF estimates that 12 million children in sub-Saharan Africa have lost at least one parent to AIDS as of 2006. By 2010 that number will likely reach 15.7 million.

- In its *U.S. Cancer Statistics: 2004 Incidence and Mortality* report (published in 2007), the National Program of Cancer Registries reports that 3,850 American women died of cervical cancer that year.

- According to Family Health International, 250,000 women world-wide die of cervical cancer each year.

- According to the CDC, 20 to 40 percent of women with chlamydia and 10 to 40 percent of women with gonorrhea may develop pelvic inflammatory disease (PID) if they do not receive adequate treatment. Tubal scarring associated with PID can lead to infertility for 20 percent of affected women.

- An article in the March 2007 issue of the *American Journal of Obstetrics and Gynecology* reported that the annual cost of HPV-related cervical diseases in the United States may be as high as $4.6 billion.

- The *Guttmacher Policy Review* reports that without prenatal intervention, one-third of babies born to HIV-positive women will become infected.

- An April 2008 University of Louisville study links HPV with lung cancer.

- According to UNAIDS, 2.1 million people died as a result of AIDS in 2007. Of those deaths, 76 percent happened in sub-Saharan Africa.

- Family Health International reports that between 55 and 85 percent of women with pelvic inflammatory disease (a common side effect of gonorrhea and chlamydia) will become infertile if they do not receive proper treatment.

Solutions to Prevent Sexually Transmitted Diseases
- According to the Guttmacher Institute:
  - Approximately 29 percent of girls with at least eight years of education use contraception, compared to only 7 percent who were in school three or fewer years.
  - Studies in Kenya, Uganda, and South Africa have found that male circumcision reduces a man's chance of contracting HIV by between 51 and 60 percent.

- According to the Centers for Disease Control and Prevention, the HPV vaccine protects against the two strains of HPV that cause 70 percent of cervical cancer cases.

- According to UNAIDS:
  - The number of people with HIV in low- and medium-income countries who have received antiretroviral treatments has increased five times between 2003 and 2006.
  - Approximately three hundred thousand deaths are avoided each year as a result of HIV treatment.
  - In 2006, more than 70 percent of people who were medically eligible for antiretrovirals lacked access to these drugs.
  - The cost of preventing and treating HIV worldwide in 2015 will be $54 billion.
  - By the end of 2006, more than 2 million people in low- and middle-income countries were undergoing antiretroviral therapy to treat HIV.

- A 2004 poll by the Kaiser Family Foundation, the Kennedy School of Government at Harvard University, and National Public Radio found that 93 percent of parents whose children have taken sexual education courses believe the classes were somewhat or very helpful.

- The organization AVERT reports that in March 2007 a congressionally mandated evaluation of abstinence-only programs found that students who take part in those programs have virtually the same rates of unprotected sex and abstinence as students who do not take part.

- According to AVERT, President George W. Bush's 2007 budget included $204 million for abstinence-only education programs.

- A 2007 study by the National Campaign to Prevent Teen and Unplanned Pregnancy concluded that abstinence-only programs do not delay the age at which adolescents have sexual intercourse. In contrast, the study found that two-thirds of the sexual education programs that combine abstinence education with information on contraception do significantly reduce the rate of unprotected sex and delay initial sexual experiences.

Organizations to Contact

The editors have compiled the following list of organizations concerned with the issues debated in this book. The descriptions are derived from materials provided by the organizations. All have publications or information available for interested readers. The list was compiled on the date of publication of the present volume; the information provided here may change. Be aware that many organizations take several weeks or longer to respond to inquiries, so allow as much time as possible.

Alive and Well AIDS Alternatives
11684 Ventura Blvd., Studio City, CA 91604
(818) 780-1875
fax: (818) 780-7093
e-mail: info@aliveandwell.org
Web site: www.aliveandwell.org

Alive and Well AIDS Alternatives presents information that questions the validity of many of the common assumptions about HIV and AIDS, including the accuracy of HIV tests and the effectiveness of AIDS drug treatments. The organization's Web site features information on whether a link exists between HIV and AIDS and also addresses facts and myths about AIDS drugs.

American Foundation for AIDS Research (AmFAR)
120 Wall St., 13th Fl., New York, NY 10005-3908
(212) 806-1600
fax: (212) 806-1601
e-mail: information@amfar.org
Web site: www.amfar.org

AmFAR is a nonprofit organization that supports HIV/AIDS research, treatment, education, and AIDS prevention. Its mission is to prevent HIV infection and to protect the human rights of everyone affected by the epidemic. The organization publishes a twice yearly newsletter, a quarterly report on HIV/AIDS in Asia and the Pacific, an annual report, and several issue briefs.

American Social Health Association
PO Box 13827, Research Triangle Park, NC 27709
(919) 361-8400
fax: (919) 361-8425
e-mail: info@ashastd.org
Web site: www.ashastd.org

The American Social Health Association is a nonprofit organization that works to improve public health outcomes and is a leading authority on information pertaining to STDs. Facts and statistics about STDs are available on its Web site. The organization's publications include *HPV in Perspective* and *Managing Herpes*.

Canadian AIDS Society (CAS)
190 O'Connor St., Ste. 800, Ottawa, ON K2P 2R3 Canada
(613) 230-3580 or (800) 499-1986
fax: (613) 563-4998
e-mail: casinfo@cdnaids.ca
Web site: www.cdnaids.ca

CAS is a national coalition of more than 125 community-based AIDS organizations. The society is dedicated to improving the lives of people living with HIV/AIDS and strengthening Canada's response to the epidemic. CAS publishes position papers, including *HIV Vaccines*, fact sheets, and reports.

Centers for Disease Control and Prevention (CDC)
Sexually Transmitted Diseases
Mailstop E11, 1600 Clifton Rd., Atlanta, GA 30333
(800) 232-4636 or (800) 311-3435
Web site: www.cdc.gov/std

The CDC is one of the major components of the Department of Health and Human Services. Its purpose is to lead public health efforts to prevent and control the spread of infectious and chronic diseases. Its section on STDs provides information on various diseases, including fact sheets and statistics, as well as links to publications.

Concerned Women for America (CWA)
1015 Fifteenth St. NW, Ste. 1100, Washington, DC 20005
(202) 488-7000

fax: (202) 488-0806

Web site: www.cwfa.org

CWA aims to promote biblical values throughout society in order to reverse the decline in America's moral values. CWA supports abstinence-only sexual education and questions the efficacy of condoms in preventing STDs. The organization publishes the magazine *Family Voice*, brochures, and articles, including "Abstinence Makes Sense: A Common Sense Rationale."

Family Health International (FHI)

PO Box 13950, Research Triangle Park, NC 27709

(919) 544-7040

fax: (919) 544-7261

Web site: www.fhi.org

The mission of FHI is to improve public health throughout the world through research and education. The organization works with research institutions, government organizations, and the private sector to achieve this goal. FHI also aims to prevent the spread of STDs and to provide care for people affected by those diseases. Books and reports are available on its Web site, including "Family Planning and the Prevention of Mother-to-Child Transmission of HIV."

Family Research Council (FRC)

801 G St. NW, Washington, DC 20001

(202) 393-2100

fax: (202) 393-2134

Web site: www.frc.org

The FRC develops public policy that upholds the institutions of marriage and family; among the issues it supports is abstinence-only education. Publications on AIDS and abstinence-only education are available on its Web site, including "Why Wait: The Benefits of Abstinence Until Marriage."

Gay Men's Health Crisis (GMHC)

119 W. Twenty-fourth St., New York, NY 10011

(212) 367-1000

Web site: www.gmhc.org

The GMHC is an organization that helps lead the fight against AIDS. It aims to reduce the spread of HIV; improve the health and independence of people with HIV; and ensure that the prevention, treatment, and cure of HIV remains a national priority. Educational materials are provided for sale on its Web site.

Guttmacher Institute
125 Maiden Lane, 7th Fl., New York, NY 10038
(800) 355-0244
fax: (212) 248-1951
Web site: www.guttmacher.org

The mission of the institute is to use public education, policy analysis, and social science research to promote sound policy and create new ideas about sexual health. It aims to improve access to information about STDs. The organization publishes the periodicals *Perspectives on Sexual and Reproductive Health, International Family Planning Perspectives*, and the *Guttmacher Policy Review*. Its Web site features a section on STDs that includes fact sheets, policy briefs, articles, and reports, including *Adding It Up: The Benefits of Investing in Sexual and Reproductive Health Care.*

International AIDS Society (IAS)
Ave. Louis Casaï 71, PO Box 20, Cointrin, Geneva, Switzerland
+41 22 710 0800
fax: +41 22 710 0899
e-mail: info@iasociety.org
Web site: www.iasociety.org

The IAS is a worldwide independent association of HIV/AIDS professionals who are working to prevent, treat, and control the epidemic. The society organizes the International AIDS Conference. Publications include a newsletter and annual report.

Sex Information and Educational Council of the United States (SIECUS)
90 John St., Ste. 704, New York, NY 10038
(212) 819-9770
fax: (212) 819-9776
Web site: www.siecus.org

SIECUS is an organization that provides information for parents, health professionals, educators, and communities in order to ensure that everybody receives comprehensive information about sexuality. It also works to have sound public policy developed on sexuality-related issues. The council publishes the quarterly journal *Siecus Report*, fact sheets, and newsletters.

World Health Organization (WHO)
Avenue Appia 20, 1211 Geneva 27, Switzerland
+41 22 791 2111
fax: +41 22 791 3111
e-mail: info@who.int
Web site: www.who.int

The World Health Organization is the specialized health agency of the United Nations. The objective of WHO is to help all people achieve the highest possible level of health. Its Web site has links to fact sheets and publications about HIV and AIDS, including "Taking Stock: HIV in Children" and "Sexual and Reproductive Health and HIV/AID."

For Further Reading

Books

David Barlow, Ali Mears, and Dip Gum, *Sexually Transmitted Infections: The Facts.* Oxford, UK: Oxford University Press, 2006. The authors use cases drawn from real patients to provide useful facts about STDs.

Richard P. Barth, *Reducing the Risk: Building Skills to Prevent Pregnancy, STD and HIV.* Scotts Valley, CA: ETR Associates, 2004. This book provides statistics and lessons that teenagers can use to lower their risk of acquiring an STD.

Garson J. Claton, ed., *AIDS in Africa: A Pandemic on the Move.* New York: Novinka, 2006. Contributors to this anthology explore how AIDS has affected Africa's families, economy, and agriculture.

Jonathan Engel, *The Epidemic: A Global History of AIDS.* New York: Smithsonian/Collins, 2006. The author looks at various aspects of the AIDS epidemic, such as its political and economic consequences, its spread throughout the world, and ways to control the virus.

Michelle M. Houle, *AIDS in the 21st Century: What You Should Know,* Berkeley Heights, NJ: Enslow, 2003. A detailed description of the AIDS epidemic, along with a glossary and reading list.

Miranda Hunter and William Hunter, *Staying Safe: A Teen's Guide to Sexually Transmitted Diseases.* Philadephia: Mason Crest, 2005. The transmittal, symptoms, and treatment of major STDs are detailed in this book, along with information on contraception.

Susan Hunter, *AIDS in America.* New York: Palgrave Macmillan, 2006. The author argues that AIDS is becoming more common and deadlier and faults U.S. policies for these changes in the epidemic.

Susan Hunter, *Black Death: AIDS in Africa.* Basingstoke, UK: Palgrave Macmillan, 2003. The author presents the argument that Western exploitation has led to the AIDS epidemic in Africa and explores ways tosolve the crisis.

Beryl Leach, Joan E. Paluzzi, and Paula Munderi, *Prescription for Healthy Development: Increasing Access to Medicines.* London: Earthscan, 2005. The authors of this book present official UN strategy on how to make AIDS medicines more available and affordable in developing countries.

Donald E. Morisky, ed., *Overcoming AIDS: Lessons Learned from Uganda.* Greenwich, CT: Information Age, 2006. The authors in this book write about AIDS orphans and explore how researchers and policy makers are seeking to improve life for these children.

Alvin Silverstein, Virginia Silverstein, and Laura Silverstein Nunn, *The STDs Update.* Berkeley Heights, NJ: Enslow Elementary, 2006. This book covers syphilis, herpes, and other STDs.

M. Monica Sweeney and Rita Kirwan Grisman, *Condom Sense: A Guide to Sexual Survival in the New Millennium.* New York: Lantern, 2005. The authors explore how condom use can protect people from contracting AIDS.

Sabrina Weill, *The Real Truth About Teens and Sex: From Hooking Up to Friends with Benefits—What Teens Are Thinking, Doing, and Talking About, and How to Help Them Make Smart Choices.* New York: Berkeley, 2005. A teen-magazine editor reveals teenagers' thoughts on their sex lives, peer pressure, and sexual education.

Periodicals

Lawrence K. Altman, "Doctors Support a Childhood Vaccine for a Sex-Related Virus," *New York Times,* October 28, 2005.

Lawrence K. Altman, "Study Finds That Teenage Virginity Pledges Are Rarely Kept," *New York Times,* March 10, 2004.

Michael Applebaum, "Life Gard: With Roots in Public-Health Policy and the Touchy Topic of Teen Sexuality, Gardasil Has Become a Hot-Button Issue. But for this Marketer, the Only Real Issue Is Helping Women Avoid Cancer," *Brandweek,* October 8, 2007.

Bob Barr, "Don't Mandate New Vaccine," *Atlanta Journal-Constitution,* February 14, 2007. www.conservative.org/columnists/barr/070214bb.htm.

Henry H. Bauer, "The Mystery of HIV/AIDS," *Quadrant,* July-August 2006.

Alicia M. Bell, "Hold the Hype on HPV," *Women's Health Activist,* May-June 2007.

Laura Billings, "Speaking of Sex," *Mpls. St. Paul Magazine,* October 2007. www.mspmag.com/health/fitforlife/78349-1.asp.

Heather Boonstra, "Comprehensive Approach Needed to Combat Sexually Transmitted Infections Among Youth," *Guttmacher Report on Public Policy,* March 2004.

Jane E. Brody, "Abstinence-Only: Does It Work?" *New York Times,* June 1, 2004.

Christianity Today, "'Safe Sex' for the Whole Nation," April 2007.

Kathy Clay-Little, "In the Real World, the Facts About Sex Are Necessary," *San Antonio Express-News,* October 8, 2007.

Stacey Colino, "The Sneaky Threat to Your Fertility," *Cosmopolitan,* April 2007.

Dawn Rae Downton, "On Guard: Women's Health Activists Are Skeptical About a Federal Plan to Vaccinate Girls as Young as Nine with Gardasil," *Herizons,* Fall 2007.

Helen Epstein, "The Fidelity Fix," *New York Times Magazine,* June 13, 2004.

J. Dennis Fortenberry, "The Limits of Abstinence-Only in Preventing Sexually Transmitted Infections," *Journal of Adolescent Health,* 2005. www.gprhe.org/fortenberry.pdf.

Nancy Gibbs, "Defusing the War over the 'Promiscuity Vaccine,'" *Time,* June 21, 2006. www.time.com/time/nation/article/0,85 99,1206813,00.html.

Global Agenda, "The Chinese Disease? The Rapid Spread of Syphilis in China; Concerns About China's Public Health," January 14, 2007.

Ellen Goodman, "A Dose of Reality on HPV Vaccine," *Boston Globe,* March 2, 2007. www.boston.com/news/globe/editorial_opinion/oped/articles/2007/03/02/a_dose_of_reality_on_hpv_vaccine.

Cathy Gulli, "Our Girls Are Not Guinea Pigs," *Maclean's,* August 27, 2007.

Kim Hak-Su, "Why We Must Defeat HIV/AIDS," *UN Chronicle,* March–May 2004.

B. Denise Hawkins, "On the Frontline of the HIV/AIDS Epidemic," *Black Issues in Higher Education,* March 24, 2005.

Cristi Hegranes, "Sloganeering: For Years the City Has Been Using Racy Ads to Sell HIV Prevention. Do They Work?" *SF Weekly,* March 1, 2006. www.sfweekly.com/2006-0301/news/sloganeering.

Todd Henneman, "Sex, Lies, and Teenagers," *Advocate,* August 16, 2005.

King K. Holmes, Ruth Levine, and Marcia Weaver, "Effectiveness of Condoms in Preventing Sexually Transmitted Infections," *Bulletin of the World Health Organization,* June 2004.

Claudia Kalb and Andrew Murr, "Battling a Black Epidemic," *Newsweek,* May 15, 2006.

Nomi Levenkron, "The Legalization of Prostitution: Myth and Reality," *Hotline for Migrant Workers,* 2007. www.hotline.org.il/english/pdf/The_Legalization_Of_Prostitution_English.pdf.

Bernard Lo, "HPV Vaccines and Adolescents' Sexual Activity," *BMJ,* May 13, 2006.

Jon Mendelson, "Sex-Ed Curriculum Could Use Addition," *Tracy Press,* October 18, 2007. http://tracypress.com/content/view/11788/2244.

Donald G. McNeil, "How a Vaccine Search Ended in Triumph," *New York Times,* August 29, 2006.

New York Times, "A Vaccine to Save Women's Lives," February 6, 2007.

Kate O'Beirne, "A Mandate in Texas: The Story of Compulsory Vaccination and What It Means," *National Review,* March 5, 2007.

Katha Pollit, "Virginity or Death!" *Nation,* May 12, 2005. www.thenation.com/doc/20050530/pollitt.

Janet E. Rosenbaum, "Reborn a Virgin: Adolescents' Retracting of Virginity Pledges and Sexual Histories," *American Journal of Public Health,* vol. 96, no. 6, June 2006.

Mpho Selemogo, "The African AIDS Crisis and International Indifference," *Humanist,* January-February 2006.

Peter Sprigg, "A Promising Vaccine . . . but Gardasil Should Not Be Mandatory," *Washington Times,* July 2006.

Judith Stephenson and Angela Obasi, "HIV Risk-Reduction in Adolescents," *Lancet,* April 10, 2004.

Patricia J. Sulak, "Adolescent Sexual Health," *Journal of Family Practice,* July 2004.

Karen Testerman, "Promiscuous Plague," *World & I,* March 2004.

Suzanne Topping, "Testimony for the October 24, 2007 Senate Democratic Conference Hearing on HPV Vaccination Requirement." www.womenshealthcollaborative.org/Resoures/GardasilTestimonyWHC.pdf.

Claudia Wallis, "A Snapshot of Teen Sex," *Time,* February 7, 2005.

Claudia Wallis, "Saying Yes to the Shot," *Time,* March 19, 2007.

World & I, "STDs: Yesterday and Today," March 2004.

Web Sites

AIDS Education Global Information Service (www.aegis.com). This Web site contains more than 1 million articles on AIDS, dating back to 1981.

AIDS*info* (www.hivatis.org). A project of the U.S. Department of Health and Human Services, this Web site offers federally approved information on clinical research trials, treatment and prevention, and experimental drugs.

Global Health Facts (www.globalhealthfacts.org). This page is run by the Kaiser Family Foundation and provides worldwide data on HIV and AIDS.

Kaiser Network (www.kaisernetwork.org). This page, operated by the Kaiser Family Foundation, features reports on HIV/AIDS and other STDs and links to webcasts.

Medline Plus: Sexually Transmitted Diseases (www.nlm.nih.gov/medlineplus/sexuallytransmitteddiseases.html). This Web site, run by the U.S. National Library of Medicine and the National

Institutes of Health, provides news and information on STDs. It also includes links to research, statistics, and articles on diagnosis and prevention.

National Institutes of Health: Sexuality Transmitted Diseases (http://health.nih.gov/result.asp/588). Operated by the National Institutes of Health, this site provides links to information on STDs from several Web sites, including the National Institute of Allergy and Infectious Diseases and the National Institute on Drug Abuse.

Index

A

AARP, 57

ABC campaign, in Uganda, 8

Abortion, parental notification laws on, 24

Abstinence-only sex education, 8–9
  contributes to the spread of STDs, 11–17
  discourages use of contraception, 81
  funding for, 79
  has reduced teen sexual activity, 23

African Americans
  increase in HIV infections among, 38
  prevalence of STDs among, 53

AIDS/HIV
  assistance to developing countries for response to, 8–9
  crack cocaine use and, 28
  deaths from, 41
  male-to-female vs. female-to-male transmission of, 28
  presence of other STDs and susceptibility to, 29
  prevalence in India, 33

Alcohol, STDs and, 53–55

Amebiasis, 40

American Civil Liberties Union (ACLU), 80

American Journal of Public Health, 42

American Medical Association (AMA), 83

Anal sex
  among virginity pledgers, 74–75
  prevalence in use of protection during, 17
  risk of transmitting HIV by, 40–41
  virginity pledgers are less likely to engage in, 67–68

AVERT, 7

B

Bajko, Matthew S., 43

Bearman, Peter, 16, 66, 68, 69, 71

Beilenson, Peter L., 30–31

Berry, Steve, 7–8

Blanco, Kathleen, 80

Bor, Jonathan, 26

Brewer, Toya, 30

Brown, Terry, 28

Brückner, Hannah, 66, 68, 69, 71

Burbank, Dee, 83

Bush administration, abstinence-only programs and, 12, 17

Picture Credits

About the Editors

Lauri S. Friedman earned her bachelor's degree in religion and political science from Vassar College in 1999. Her studies there focused on political Islam, and she produced a thesis on the Islamic Revolution in Iran titled *Neither West, Nor East, but Islam*. She also holds a preparatory degree in flute performance from the Manhattan School of Music.

She is the founder of LSF Editorial, a writing and editing outfit in San Diego, CA. Her clients include Greenhaven Press, for whom she has edited numerous titles on gay marriage, drug abuse, the war on terror, Iraq, pandemics, genetic engineering, and more. A former in-house senior editor at Greenhaven, she helped conceive of and design the *Introducing Issues with Opposing Viewpoints* series.

Friedman lives in Ocean Beach, San Diego, with her husband, Randy, and their yellow lab, Trucker. In her spare time she enjoys pottery, making music, taking Trucker to the beach, and traveling.

Jennifer L. Skancke lives and works in San Francisco. Aside from writing, she loves reading, HBO programming, learning Italian, hiking, camping, traveling, and laughing with friends.